# Inked
## in
# India

Also by the author

*Navaratri: When Devi Comes Home*
(co-edited by Anuradha Goyal)

*The Bhagavad Gita for Millennials*

*Manmatha Nath Dutt: Translator Extraordinaire*

*On the Trail of the Black: Tracking Corruption*
(co-edited by Kishore Arun Desai)

# Inked in India

## FOUNTAIN PENS AND A STORY OF MAKE AND UNMAKE

### BIBEK DEBROY

WITH **SOVAN ROY**

RUPA

Published by
Rupa Publications India Pvt. Ltd 2022
7/16, Ansari Road, Daryaganj
New Delhi 110002

*Sales Centres:*
Allahabad  Bengaluru  Chennai
Hyderabad  Jaipur  Kathmandu
Kolkata  Mumbai

ISBN: 978-93-552-0564-3

First impression 2022

10 9 8 7 6 5 4 3 2 1

The moral right of the authors has been asserted.

Printed in India

*For all those who treasure*
*Indian fountain pens*

# CONTENTS

# INTRODUCTION

This is an unusual book written by two authors who came together by accident. Bibek Debroy is an economist; Sovan Roy specializes in science and technology. Both happen to be Bengalis. But that is a coincidence. Both were born in, what was then, undivided Assam—Bibek Debroy in Shillong and Sovan Roy in Guwahati. That too is incidental. What is not incidental is that both have a passion for fountain pens, especially those that are Indian. As is customary with all collectors, the two authors first met when they started to exchange surplus pens from each other's collections. 'Here is a Mebsons. Do you have a Bharati?' stuff like that. It was a remarkable coincidence that in 2019, both authors independently rediscovered Dr Radhika Nath Saha (1870–1933). Bibek Debroy discovered Dr Saha's 1911 book and wrote an article on him. Having studied in Benares (now Varanasi) at the Banaras Hindu University (BHU), Sovan Roy wrote an entire book on Saha, *Radhika Nath Saha: Unsung Hero of Indian Fountain Pen.*[1]

In the midst of the Covid-19 pandemic, the seeds of the book were sown. Beyond the odd journalistic piece here and there, there has been no satisfactory account on the history of Indian fountain pen, ink and incidental manufactures. There is, of course, the very useful online chronicle that Chawm Ganguly writes, named 'Inked Happiness'. Simultaneously, there

---

[1]Roy, Sovan, *Radhika Nath Saha: Unsung Hero of Indian Fountain Pen,* Kabitika, 2019.

has been a resurgence of interest in Indian fountain pens and ink, though that is still limited to those in the know and has not necessarily percolated to the general population. This book, the first of its kind, serves two purposes: (a) It is a history of fountain pen (and ink) making in India. (b) Using fountain pens as a case study, it documents how faulty economic policies messed up make in India. It is by no means our case that we have listed every manufacturer. By virtue of both of us being Bengalis, there is probably a bias towards those from the eastern parts of the country. But that is not a deliberate bias. We hope that this book is a start and there will be others, with more comprehensive compilations.

Given the paucity of information, it was also not an easy book to write. Along the way, as authors, we accumulated several debts. If we fail to acknowledge some, it is an act of inadvertent omission, not advertent commission. However, we have also gained insights from conversations with manufacturers who produce fountain pens even today. Lest we be accused of bias, those names have not been mentioned.

In alphabetical order, using first names, we are indebted to Aditya Sinha, Aniruddha Chakraborty, Apurba Kumar Panda, Chandranath Chattopadhyay, Chawm Ganguly, Donesh Jain, Gautam Chikermane, Mahuya Hom Choudhury, Nikhil Ranjan, Paramita Saha, Sangeeta Mitra, Sajish Nair, Samir Saran, Soumen Nath, Subhajeet Saha and Vikram Doraiswami. The photographs used in this book were taken by Bibek Debroy and Tapash Ghosh, and we thank the latter for making the book come vividly alive. We thank all those who collect Indian fountain pens and write about them. Who else can a book like this be dedicated to?

Bibek Debroy and Sovan Roy
Delhi and Kolkata, July 2022

# 1

## STORIES OF PEN AND INK

The National Mission for Manuscripts was established in 2003. 'The Mission has the mandate of identifying, documenting, conserving and making accessible the manuscript heritage of India.'[1] There are an estimated 35 million manuscripts in India, not all of which have yet been catalogued; so, official figures are smaller. 'A manuscript is a handwritten composition on paper, bark, cloth, metal, palm leaf or any other material dating back at least seventy-five years that has significant scientific, historical or aesthetic value.'[2] Traditionally, knowledge came down through oral transmission. Writing is comparatively of recent vintage. The oldest surviving manuscripts go back to the ninth century CE. Manuscripts, sometimes illuminated, were written on various materials, but our subject is the writing implement or writing instrument one wrote with, not the material out of which manuscripts were made. This book does not document an evolution of writing

---

[1]National Mission for Manuscripts, https://bit.ly/3wJBngy. Accessed on 24 May 2022.
[2]'What Is Manuscript?', National Mission for Manuscripts, https://bit.ly/3mnGHBg. Accessed on 7 June 2022.

technology but discusses India's economic transition and its fountain pens and inks.

As is only to be expected, ink is older than pens, not to speak of fountain pens. Across old civilizations—India, Egypt, China, Rome—ink, based on lampblack and pigments with plant, animal and mineral origins, was used. The history of those experiments and innovations is often forgotten. Something like D.C. Sircar's *Indian Epigraphy*, deserves far better dissemination.

> Palmyra leaves, separated from the lengthwise joint in the middle and cut at both ends according to the required size, were used for writing letters as well as manuscripts of literary works in Sanskrit and other languages [...] In North India, the general practice was to write on the leaves with pen and ink, while, in the South, the letters were incised on the leaves with a sharp-pointed needle and were made black by besmearing ink on the writing.[3]

In Sanskrit, the most common word for ink is *masi*. This ink was made from lampblack or charcoal, mixed with gum, sugar and other ingredients. The process for making permanent and non-washable ink went something like this: the resin of the pipal tree was ground and mixed with water, which was then boiled and mixed with ground borax and *lodhra*[4] and finally strained through a cloth. To impart black colour, lampblack was added. Mixing vermilion made the ink red. Other hues of ink were green, yellow, gold and silver.

---

[3]Sircar, D.C., *Indian Epigraphy*, Motilal Banarsidass Publication, Delhi, 1965.
[4]A tree whose bark was used for dyeing

The writing on cloth and birch bark referred to by Nearchus and Curtius suggests that ink was used by the Indians in the 4th century BC The word *lipi*, from the root *lip*, found in Panini's grammar (c. 5th century B.C.) and the inscriptions of Asoka (c. 272–232 B.C.) points to the same conclusion.[5]

## Of *Kalama* and Quill

So, what was ink applied with in the old civilizations of India?

*Lekhani* (literally 'the instrument for writing') is a general name for the stylus, pencil, brush, pen, etc. *Varnika*, mentioned in early Indian literature, was a wooden pen, pointed at the end without a slit. It was used by young learners at the elementary schools. *Isika* was originally a pen made of reed or bamboo branch and was used by the copyists of manuscripts.[6]

The quill pen was not as ubiquitous in India as it was in other parts of the world. The writing instrument is a function of what one is writing on. So, if one is writing on parchment or vellum, both of which are animal skins, a quill pen might be better, as was the case in Europe. But this is not necessarily so if one is writing on bark, cloth or palm leaf. When paper made from wood pulp became the writing material, the quill pen declined in importance, though some calligraphers still swear by it.

---

[5]Sircar, D.C., *Indian Epigraphy*, Motilal Banarsidass Publication, Delhi, 1965.
[6]Ibid.

No one can possibly date the use of a quill pen. In Sanskrit, the word *patatri* means a bird, or something that flies, from the verbal root *pat*, meaning 'to fly'. That word is cognate with the Latin word *penna* or *pinna*—the wing on the body of a flying creature—a feather. When we use the term 'pen', we implicitly acknowledge a pen's antecedents in a quill made from a feather.

Whenever quill pens are mentioned, Isidore of Seville (sixth and seventh century CE) is invariably quoted. He wrote a book called *Etymologiae* or *Origines*, documenting the etymology of various words. As Isidore of Seville wrote in this oft-quoted Latin phrase, '*instrumenta scribae, calamus et penna: sed calamus arboris est, penna avis* (the scribe's tools are calamus and penna; but the calamus is the tree and penna is the bird).' However, he wrote a little bit more about reed pens and quills:

> The scribe's tools are the reed-pen and the quill, for by these the words are fixed onto the page. A reed-pen is from a tree; a quill is from a bird [...] The reed-pen (*calamus*) is so called because it places liquid, whence among sailors 'to place' is *calare* [...] A quill (*pinna*) is so called from 'hanging' (*pendere*), that is, flying, for it comes, as we have said, from birds.[7]

This is interesting because many people in India will refer to a pen not as *lekhani*, *varnika* or *ishika*, but as *kalam(a)*. Sircar explains this in his book, 'The word *kalama* may have been adopted in Sanskrit from Greek through Arabic. But it is recognized as a Sanskrit word in the Sanskrit–Chinese lexicons

---

[7]Barney, Stephen A., et al. (eds), *The Etymologies of Isidore of Seville*, Cambridge University Press, 2006.

of the 8th century A.D.[8] This only confirms that in India, we traditionally used a *kalam(a)* (as in a reed pen), not pen (as in a quill).

But in many parts of the world, the quill had its day. To set matters in perspective, the original writing implement might have been a brush. However, at some point in time, it became a pen with a hard tip. That pen might have been a reed pen, where a reed or a strip of bamboo used to be sharpened so that the point acted as a nib. It might also have been a quill pen, where a feather was sharpened to achieve the same purpose.[9] Eventually, at some point, both the reed pen and the quill pen yielded to the dip pen, with a nib made of metal and a holder made of bone, plastic, glass and, especially, metal.

The Magna Carta Libertatum was signed at Runnymede in 1215 and was written with a quill pen made from the feather of a large bird, probably a goose. King John didn't actually sign it—he put his seal to it.[10] Many years before the Magna Carta, most of the Dead Sea Scrolls had been written with a quill. Some seem to have been written with a reed pen. Many years after the Magna Carta, Thomas Jefferson's Draft Declaration of Independence and the United States (US) Constitution were both written with quill pens. In deference, the US Supreme Court still has a practice of displaying quill pens, though the

---

[8]Sircar, D.C., *Indian Epigraphy*, Motilal Banarsidass Publication, Delhi, 1965.
[9]The quill pen has left a legacy in the expression 'pen knife', though there are some differences between a classic quill knife and a pen knife.
[10]In 2015, celebrating 800 years of the Magna Carta, the Royal Mint made an elementary mistake by minting a coin that showed King John holding a quill in his right hand and the Magna Carta in his left.

practice of the judiciary actually using quill pens died out in the 1920s. However, even now, an explanation of how the US Supreme Court works says:

> Opening formalities link the current day to the past. The Marshal or Deputy Marshal acts as Crier. A few minutes before 10 a.m., Crier and Clerk, formally dressed in cutaways, go to their desks below the ends of the high bench. Pencils, pens, papers, briefs, and a pewter mug of water are at each Justice's place [...] Before each chair at the four counsel tables, lie white goose-quill pens, neatly crossed; most lawyers appear before the Court only once, and gladly take the quills home as souvenirs.[11]

The use of the quill pen declined over time. However, during the centuries when it held sway, books that taught children how to write also taught them how to make quills. One such book, written entirely in verse, is dated circa 1590 and is titled *Rules Made by E.B. for His Children to Learne to Write Bye.* Rare copies exist in some libraries. An essay by Martina Wernli quotes from this book:

> To chuse your quill
> Take quill of a goose that is some what rounde,
> The thirde or fourth in wynge to be fownde:
> And if at some tyme of those ye do want,
> Take pinion as next when Rauens quilie is skant,
> And ryue it iust in the backe, as may bee.[12]

---

[11]'How The Court Works—Oral Argument', Supreme Court Historical Society, https://bit.ly/3lDVojo. Accessed on 24 May 2022.
[12]Wernli, Martina, 'From Geese to Steel: Stories about the Quill and the Nib Pen', in, Rosenhaft, Eve, Helga Mullneritsch and Annie Mattsson

The English is so archaic that it almost needs a translation. The goose was the favoured bird for the requisite feather, preferably a plump goose. Naturally, large birds led to better quills. But not all quills came from goose feathers. There were other birds too, depending on availability and intended use—swan, crow, eagle, owl, hawk, turkey and even, as the quote suggests, a raven. If you wanted larger letters, you chose a swan's feather, though those were expensive. If you wanted fine lettering, you chose a crow's feather. Good quills came from live birds, preferably when they moulted every year. Only the first five primary feathers—including the pinion, which is the outermost primary flight feather—could be used. E.B. exhibited a preference for the third or the fourth.

For a quill pen, the feathers from the left wing were preferred for a right-hander and the feathers from the right wing for a left-hander. In a similar vein, fountain pen aficionados will know that some pen manufacturers make left-handed nibs these days for left-handers. Too much can be made of this though. Because English is written from left to right and because ink takes time to dry, left-handers may end up smudging the paper. That doesn't have anything to do with the nib, unless one is using a soft or flexible nib, in which case a left-hander pushes a fountain pen while writing instead of pulling it. Such exceedingly soft and flexible nibs are rare now, making the discussion unnecessary.

The Industrial Revolution changed matters. Writing with quills and making quills was not easy, but quills were elastic. Initial steel nibs were not. As the Industrial Revolution

(eds), *The Materiality of Writing: Manuscript Practices in the Age of Print*, Uppsala University Press, 2019.

progressed in Britain, the technology for making steel nibs improved and these nibs, too, became elastic, cheap and competitive vis-à-vis quills. After all, quill feathers were imported from the Netherlands, Germany, Russia and Poland. This was 'Make in England' at work, especially concentrated in a place like Birmingham. The transition is reflected in as unlikely a place as Herman Melville's *Moby-Dick*, published in 1851, bang in the middle of the transition.

> But Stubb, he eats the whale by its own light, does he? And that is adding insult to injury, is it? Look at your knife-handle, there, my civilized and enlightened gourmand dining off that roast beef, what is that handle made of? What but the bones of the brother of the very ox you are eating? And what do you pick your teeth with, after devouring that fat goose? With a feather of the same fowl. And with what quill did the Secretary of the Society for the Suppression of Cruelty to Ganders formally indite his circulars? It is only within the last month or two that that society passed a resolution to patronize nothing but steel pens.[13]

These steel nibs edged out quills and led to dip pens, which had to be periodically dipped in an inkpot. Eventually, the dip pen yielded to a fountain pen, equipped with an internal reservoir of ink. Simultaneously, in India, as the country moved towards Independence, the world of dip pens yielded to the world of fountain pens.

---

[13]Melville, Herman, 'Chapter 65', *Moby-Dick; or, The Whale*, Harper & Brothers, 1851. The Society for the Suppression of Cruelty to Ganders, mentioned in the quote, is a fictional society.

## A Pen with a Reservoir

Trying to precisely date the advent of the fountain pen is impossible. There are references to an Islamic prototype, circa tenth century CE.[14] Leonardo da Vinci's sketches show a kind of pen with a reservoir. On 5 August 1663, Samuel Pepys wrote in his diary, 'This evening came a letter about business from Mr. Coventry, and with it a silver pen he promised me to carry inke in, which is very necessary.'[15] Ergo, in the seventeenth century, a kind of silver pen with an internal reservoir existed.

A widely circulated myth about Nicolas Bion (1652–1733), chief instrument-maker to the French king, is as follows: (a) Bion made fountain pens; (b) he got a patent; (c) five samples of his pens survive in various museums. All three statements are possibly false. Nicolas Bion made, or designed, no fountain pens. He did write a book in French, published in 1709 and translated into English as *The Construction and Principal Uses of Mathematical Instruments*. The English translation by Edmund Stone was published in 1723. In the book, he mentioned fountain pens and drew a picture, but he did not claim that he invented them:

> When the aforementioned Pen is to be used, the Cover G [*sic*] must be taken off, and the Pen a little shaken, in order to make the Ink run freely. *Note*, If the Porte-Craion

---

[14]Bosworth, C.E., 'A Mediaeval Islamic Prototype of the Fountain Pen?', *Journal of Semitic Studies*, Vol. 26, No. 1, 1981, pp. 229–34, https://bit.ly/3NBpnEf. Accessed on 7 June 2022.

[15]'Diary Entries from August 1663 | Saturday 1 August 1663', The Diary of Samuel Pepys, https://bit.ly/3sPjjjF. Accessed on 24 May 2022.

does not stop the Mouth of the Piece F [*sic*], the Air, by its Pressure, will cause the Ink all to run out at once.[16]

During Bion's time, patenting had not started. It was too early for him to go around patenting fountain pens. What of the Bion pens that exist in museums? Those actually date from the early nineteenth century and are Bion-type pens, not pens made by Bion.

Several patents were registered in the nineteenth century— for nibs, holders for nibs, the reservoir, the feed (which links the nib and the reservoir) and the filling mechanism—but mass manufacture only began after the first decade of the twentieth century. Between 1922 and 1970, Richmal Crompton wrote a succession of *Just William* stories. Those early ones, such as the 1922 *Just William*, talked about inkpots and blotting paper—the world of dip pens.[17] In later *Just William* stories, fountain pens appeared.

Quotes from two famous authors illustrate how perceptions about the fountain pen changed. The first is by Mark Twain (1835–1910): 'None of us can have as many virtues as the fountain-pen, or half its cussedness; but we can try.'[18] This was part of the 'Pudd'nhead Wilson's New Calendar' and featured in *Following the Equator*, written in 1897. The fountain pen

---

[16]Bion, Nicolas, *The Construction and Principal Uses of Mathematical Instruments*, H.W. for John Senex, 1723, Internet Archive, https://bit.ly/3GepB27. Accessed on 24 May 2022. The French title of this work was *Traité de la construction et des principaux usages des instruments de mathématique*.

[17]There were a total of 39 *Just William* books.

[18]Harnsberger, Caroline Thomas (ed.), *Mark Twain at Your Fingertips: A Book of Quotations*, Dover Publications, 2009.

had made its appearance but its performance could be erratic, or so Twain thought. However, Twain did not have as dismal a view of fountain pens as that oft-cited quote might make you think. He used pens from Paul E. Wirt, which was among the first manufacturers of fountain pens, established in 1894. In the first couple of decades, it was far ahead of brands like Parker or Waterman. The company diversified and eventually died out. Wirt quoted Twain's certification in its advertisements: '[...] a great pen [...] the only fountain pen in the world that can be left open by the week without its' drying up.'[19] In 1886, Twain wrote to Wirt, 'With a single Wirt pen I have earned the family's living for many years. With two, I could have grown rich.'[20]

By Graham Greene's time (1904–91), the fountain pen was part of a writer's persona. Therefore, in an interview to the *International Herald Tribune* in October 1977, Greene said, 'My two fingers on a typewriter have never connected with my brain. My hand on a pen does. A fountain pen, of course. Ballpoint pens are only good for filling out forms on a plane.'[21] The span of more than 90 years between 1886 and 1977 represents the rise of the fountain pen and the beginnings of its decline.

Closer home, an anecdote from Jawaharlal Nehru's childhood is often quoted.

> One of my earliest recollections is of this temper, for I was the victim of it. I must have been five or six then.

---

[19]Ibid.

[20]Anderson, Frederick, (ed.) et al., *Mark Twain's Notebooks & Journals, Volume III (1883-1891),* University of California Press, 1980.

[21]Kelner, Stephen P., *Motivate Your Writing!,* University Press of New England, 2005.

I noticed one day two fountain-pens on his office table and I looked at them with greed. I argued with myself that father could not require both at the same time and so I helped myself to one of them. Later I found that a mighty search was being made for the lost pen and I grew frightened at what I had done, but I did not confess. The pen was discovered and my guilt proclaimed to the world. Father was very angry and he gave me a tremendous thrashing. Almost blind with pain and mortification at my disgrace, I rushed to mother, and for several days various creams and ointments were applied to my aching and quivering little body.[22]

When quoting this incident from Nehru's autobiography, no one has commented on the obvious. Born in 1889, Nehru would have been five or six in 1894 or 1895. At that time, as with Twain, a fountain pen would have been a rare and valuable possession for Motilal Nehru. By the time the autobiography was published in 1936, fountain pens had become commonplace. Which fountain pen did Motilal Nehru possess in 1894 or 1895? Versions of this incident, recounted in books meant for children, mention a shiny black fountain pen, trimmed with gold. This is imagination at work. Nehru gave us no such description. It was too early for the likes of Parker, Waterman or Pelikan. So, the pens may very well have been Wirt pens of the kind Twain used. Some Wirt pens were indeed shiny black, trimmed with gold. But these are images of much later vintage. The earliest pictures of Wirt pens, in black and white, are from advertisements circa 1905, too unclear to make out anything about them.

---

[22]Nehru, Jawaharlal, *An Autobiography*, The Bodley Head, London, 1936.

Given Motilal Nehru's background, to find out which pen he used, we should really look at English fountain pen makers. That means, in all probability, Burge, Warren and Ridgley or Mabie Todd & Bard. But Burge, Warren and Ridgley's Neptune brand fountain pen took off much later. In 1887, Mabie Todd & Bard introduced the famous Swan brand. Hence, Motilal Nehru must have, in all likelihood, possessed two Swan pens. After all, the Swan was sold as 'the pen of the British empire'. An old advertisement from 1895 mentions a price of 10 pounds and six pence for a Swan pen.[23] Using an average rate of inflation, this would add up to around 1,500 pounds today. So, each pen would cost around 150,000 rupees today. If one thinks about it this way, one can understand Motilal Nehru's anger.

[23]'English Periodical: Advertisement for Swan Fountain Pens 1895', Alamy, https://bit.ly/3HnlTnc. Accessed on 15 June 2022.

# 2

## INK AND PENS:
## DOWN TO THE 1920s

'I'll call for pen and ink, and write my mind.' William Shakespeare wrote in *Henry VI, Part I.* One does not need to quote Shakespeare to establish that inks existed before pens, of either the dip or fountain pen variety. Without splitting hairs between a gel, a sol and a solution, ink is simply a coloured solution. This colouring can be through a dye, which chemically bonds with the surface to which it is applied, or through a pigment, which does not. A purist might argue that all ink should be black. After all, through old French, late Greek or late Latin, the etymology of the term 'ink' is a dark or black fluid, obtained through a burning process. Most cultures had some form of ink, based on natural dyes and some variety of lampblack, which was meant for writing or drawing. However, such ink, in general, wasn't quite suitable for printing, which was a problem once Johannes Gutenberg invented the printing press.

In 1904, just around the time when fountain pens started to make their presence felt, a book was published on the history of ink titled *Forty Centuries of Ink*.[24] Fountain pens had arrived by 1904, but this book didn't mention them. It did mention stylo pens though (more on stylo pens later).

> Stylographic inks should not be used upon records, most of them are aniline. The absence of solid matter, which makes them desirable for the stylographic pen, unfits them for records. Never add water to ink. While an ink which has water as its base might, under certain conditions bear the addition of an amount equal to that lost by evaporation, as a rule the ink particles which have become injured will not assimilate again.[25]

Aniline ink is made from an aniline dye dissolved in alcohol with a resin used for binding. It is suitable as printing ink. In nineteenth-century Calcutta (now Kolkata), especially after the Press and Registration of Books Act of 1867, when printing and publishing exploded, almost becoming a cottage industry, printing ink was required and was produced. That aniline ink, dissolved in alcohol, sufficed for printing and even for dip pens.

However, fountain pens are different and have various conditions for the ink used. The material used in making a fountain pen, such as the body or the feed, consists of ebonite, celluloid, plastic, natural rubber and so on. These can be damaged by alcohol or any organic solvent. Contrary to the point made in the quote, fountain pen ink needs to be soluble in water. And, unlike a dip pen, where this is not an issue, ink in a fountain pen needs to flow smoothly. Ink did not need to

---

[24]Carvalho, David N., *Forty Centuries of Ink*, The Banks Law Publishing Company, New York, 1904.
[25]Ibid.

be stored or made to flow in a dip pen. Typically, a pigment cannot be used in a fountain pen because it will clog the flow and prevent capillary action.

## Tracing Indian Fountain Pen Ink

As fountain pens developed, so did fountain pen ink. Because of this process of transition, there is no simple way to identify the first manufacturer of fountain pen ink. There were several manufacturers in the second half of the nineteenth century. Diamine, which started in 1864, still makes fountain pen ink. Herbin,[26] which also continues to make fountain pen ink, traces its antecedents to 1670, though what was being manufactured then was not quite fountain pen ink.

A similar problem confronts us when we try to identify the first Indian producer of fountain pen ink. It wasn't a binary, with a neat transition from other forms of ink to fountain pen ink. With a caveat about the timeline, there was PM Bagchi and Company, from Canning Street, Calcutta, originally named Dorjipara (Darjipara) Chemical Works. PM Bagchi and Company was established in 1883, much before Luxmy or Gooptu's. In the early years, it produced aniline liquid writing ink, or so some people say—it is a contested claim. Aniline is a dye used for printing ink, not for writing ink. Therefore, in all probability, PM Bagchi and Company initially manufactured ink for printing, switching to writing ink later. In any event, it eventually released PM Bagchi's Ideal Fountain Pen Ink, available in royal blue and red, which became quite

---

[26]Herbin sealing wax was used among royalty.

popular.[27] Some years down the line, in 1931, a booklet in Bengali titled *Desher Katha: Swadeshi Shilper Talika*, listing Swadeshi industries, was published.[28] It mentions PM Bagchi as manufacturers of fountain pen ink, printing ink and ink for rubber stamps. So, clearly, PM Bagchi did eventually produce fountain pen ink, that too more than 19 varieties and colours, sold under the brand name Saraswati.

D. Waldies and Company, based in Konnagar, is said to have manufactured ink as well but this has, at best, several caveats attached.[29] David Waldie (1813–89), a chemist from Scotland, moved to India in 1853, worked for a chemical manufacturer named Malcolm and Company in Calcutta, and subsequently set up D. Waldies and Company in 1858. Waldies Compound Limited (the present name) is one of the oldest manufacturers of lead oxide and sulphuric acid. Waldie may have played a role in the introduction of chloroform as an anaesthetic for surgery before his arrival in India.[30] After Waldie's death, the ownership of the company changed. In any event, there is no hard evidence that this company ever produced any ink—fountain pen or otherwise.

---

[27]PM Bagchi and Company was incorporated in March 1945 as a private limited company.

[28]*Desher Katha: Swadeshi Shilper Talika*, Swadeshi Shilpa Prachar Samiti, Bengali year 1338. The title translates to 'An account of the country (a list of Swadeshi enterprise)'.

[29]See, for example, Roy, Sovan, *Radhika Nath Saha: Unsung Hero of Indian Fountain Pen*, Kabitika, 2019.

[30]'David Waldie - From Chloroform to Calcutta', Annet House Museum, Internet Archive | Wayback Machine, https://bit.ly/3wEPq88. Accessed on 24 May 2022.

## Dr Saha and His Innovations

In 1911, a remarkable gentleman authored a remarkable book.[31] This gentleman was Radhika Nath Saha, a doctor, as in Member of College of Physicians and Surgeons (MCPS). The book was *Romance of Pen Industries*. Dr Saha was also an inventor. Among several other things, he invented a tubular feed fountain pen and set up the Luxmy Stylo Pen Works in Benares. Dr Saha's book tells us that the first mention of a fountain pen can be found in Charles Hutton's *Mathematical and Philosophical Dictionary*, published in 1795.[32] The dictionary has a quaint definition of a fountain pen:

> The fountain-pen consists of divers [*sic*] pieces of metal, the middle piece carrying the pen, which is screwed into the inside of a small pipe; and this again is soldered into another pipe of the same size as the lid; in which lid is soldered a male screw, for screwing on the cover; as also for stopping a little hole at the place, and hindering the ink from passing through it: at the other end of the piece is a small pipe, on the outside of which may be screwed

---

[31]Saha, R.N., *Romance of Pen Industries, Being A Complete Manual for the Manufacture of Writing Materials, their History, Progress, and Effects on Human Advancement, with Special Reference to the Economics and Prosperity Problems of India*, Baptist Mission Press, Calcutta, 1911. When this book was written, it was a recommended text book for industrial schools in the United Provinces.

[32]The Saha book mentions the date of publication of 1795 for Hutton's book, though Hutton's two volumes seem to have been published in 1815. Perhaps there was an earlier edition. One copy of the supposed 1795 edition is available here: https://ebay.to/3PUdICH. Accessed on 1 June 2022.

the top cover. A portecraion [*sic*] goes in the cover, to be screwed into the last-mentioned pipe, to stop the end of the pipe into which the ink is to be poured through a funnel. To use the pen, the cover must be taken off, and the pen a little shaken, to make the ink run more freely.[33]

Except that last sentence, which makes sense even today, everything else sounds awfully complicated. Shorn of complications, a fountain pen was simply a pen with an in-built reservoir of ink, so that one didn't have to constantly dip into inkpots.

Dr Saha's achievements were nothing short of remarkable. He was born in Chinsurah and his father, Brojo Nath Saha, was a civil surgeon and linguist. When his father retired, the family settled down in Benares. Saha was a qualified doctor and could have followed his father's footsteps into government service. Instead, he opted for private practice, so that he could have free time while earning enough to pursue his commercial ventures. Recently, Sovan Roy wrote a book on Dr Saha,[34] chasing various leads, which mentions 120 patents granted on different types of fountain pens in 1911. There was obviously a lot of innovation occurring in this area back then. Coincidentally, 1911 was the year when a sailor friend gave Kyugoro Sakata, an engineer based in Hiroshima, a fountain

---

[33]Hutton, Charles, *A Mathematical and Philosophical Dictionary: Containing an Explanation of the Terms, and an Account of the Several Subjects, Comprized under the Heads Mathematics, Astronomy, and Philosophy, Both Natural and Experimental,* Cambridge University Press, 2015.

[34]Roy, Sovan, *Radhika Nath Saha: Unsung Hero of Indian Fountain Pen,* Kabitika, 2019.

pen imported from England. This led to the establishment of Sailor Pens, the first company to make fountain pens in Japan. Today, whenever Japanese fountain pen brands are mentioned, Sailor is invariably included along with Pilot and Platinum. Dr Saha, however, has been all but forgotten.

Dr Saha obtained 14 patents on fountain pens, stylo pens and automatic calendars in four countries (India, the United Kingdom [UK], Germany, the US) between 1900 and 1927. Stylo pens, or stylographic pens, was one of the types of pens he worked on, have a writing tip made of a metal tube with a wire inside regulating ink flow. Stylo pens were quite the rage throughout the first two decades of the twentieth century, until fountain pens rendered them obsolete. The contemporary ballpoint, stylus and drafting pens are descendants of stylo pens.

A patent is a form of intellectual property right protection that often builds on what has already been invented—the store of human knowledge, so to speak. A new patent cites the store of human knowledge on which the patentee has improved. The technical nomenclature is 'prior art', which is an expression for the state of existing knowledge. Even as late as the 1950s, new US patents cited Dr Saha's US patent number 962982 of 1910.[35] Depending on the country and the year, only about 5–7 per cent of patents are commercialized. In an exceptional

---

[35]'R.N. Saha, fountain pen, application filed on May 7, 1908, 962,982. Patented June 28, 1910', Patent Images, https://bit.ly/3GdHduS. Accessed on 24 May 2022; Saha, R.N., *Romance of Pen Industries, Being A Complete Manual for the Manufacture of Writing Materials, their History, Progress, and Effects on Human Advancement, with Special Reference to the Economics and Prosperity Problems of India*, Baptist Mission Press, Calcutta, 1911. This patent concerned the flow of ink in fountain pens.

example of entrepreneurship, the famous educationist and chemist, Acharya Prafulla Chandra Ray (1861–1944) established Bengal Chemicals and Pharmaceuticals in Calcutta in 1901. Dr Saha commercialized his patents along similar lines. He set up Luxmy Stylo Pen Works Company Limited in Benares in 1907, named after the location of Saha's Benares house in Luxmy Kunda. The company manufactured pens that were, 'surpassed by no other pen in quality and durability, and their price [was] much cheaper than that of any imported pens.'[36] The company also produced fountain pens. The body for a stylo pen or a nib pen was the same while the point used for writing differed; both were known as Luxmy Pens. Thus, Dr Saha should probably claim the record for producing the first fountain pen in India. Posterity never gave him due credit.

Though formally registered in 1907, the process for starting Luxmy Pens and manufacturing stylo and fountain pens was initiated in 1901. The first prototype for fountain and stylo pens—which had the same base and only their screwed in top differed—was developed by Nilmony Karmakar, a mechanic from Chandernagore (now Chandannagar). Dr Saha's factory also produced stylo and fountain pen ink. After his death, Luxmy Stylo Pen Works Company went into a gradual decline. Internally, his descendants lacked the skills. Externally, there was competition and the advent of new technology. Eventually, the enterprise fizzled out by the early 1950s. When Luxmy Pens ruled the roost, Mahatma Gandhi, Rabindranath Tagore,

---

[36]Saha, R.N., *Romance of Pen Industries, Being A Complete Manual for the Manufacture of Writing Materials, their History, Progress, and Effects on Human Advancement, with Special Reference to the Economics and Prosperity Problems of India*, Baptist Mission Press, Calcutta, 1911.

Rajendra Prasad and Maulana Abul Kalam Azad possessed these pens. Dr Saha's book documents the travails many contemporary Indian manufacturers will empathize with—the availability of finance, high customs duties and octroi, patenting costs and even labour problems.[37]

Dr Saha's intellectual pursuits were not limited to the book *Romance of Pen Industries* or patenting his pens. He wrote on the Bengali alphabet, the Brahmi script and medical science (co-authored with his father).

In a 1902 piece titled 'The Revival of Industry in India',[38] Sri Aurobindo wrote, 'I would suggest that, of the many manufactures which might be successful in India, it would be advisable to begin with those in which there is a steady local demand, such as soap, candles, glass, furniture, pen-nibs, carpets, etc., and afterwards extend the field of our operations so as to include other and more elaborate articles.' Dr Saha may not have read Sri Aurobindo, since it was not known till 1940 that Sri Aurobindo, and not the Maharaja of Baroda, had written this. But he, and others like him, did act on that philosophy.

---

[37]Ibid. 'The first factory hands, recruited from the Lucknow Railway Workshop, after a year's training and work by treadle power, demanded higher wages when the factory was equipped with engine power, struck work, and were dismissed.' In a day of eight working hours, each factory hand could produce three to six dozen finished fountain pens.

[38]Sri Aurobindo, 'The Revival of Industry in India', *Early Cultural Writings, The Complete Works of Sri Aurobindo*, Vol. 1, Sri Aurobindo Ashram Trust, 2003.

## Pen Manufacturers: India and Abroad

In passing, Dr Saha's book mentions nib factories that had been started in India: Gwalior State Nib Factory was set up in Mumbai by the Tambat Brothers and the Gujarat Nib Factory in Punjab. It also includes a list of 13 global fountain pen makers in 1911: (a) Mabie, Todd & Bard, London, with the Swan brand; (b) Waterman Pen Company, New York; (c) De La Rue, London and US, with the Nota Bene, Pelican, Onoto and Onostyle brands; (d) Jewel Pen Company, London; (e) Eagle Pencil, New York; (f) Moore's, US; (g) Dr Faber, Toledo, US; (h) A.W. Faber, US, with the Independent brand; (i) Burge, Warren and Ridgley, London; (j) Parker and Lawrence; (k) A.T. Cross, England and US; (l) Paul Ewart Bloomsbury, US; and (m) Conklin Pen Company, Toledo.

The aforementioned booklet in Bengali listing Swadeshi industries,[39] published in 1931, naturally documents developments till the end of the 1920s. For nibs and pens (which may also mean dip pens), it mentions the following: (a) F.N. Gooptu, Calcutta; (b) Calcutta Horn Manufacturing, Anand Palit Road; (c) P. Ghosh and Brothers, Calcutta; (d) Orient Nibs, Calcutta; and (e) Model Industries, Dayalbagh, Agra. In a separate listing for fountain pens, it mentions (a) Luxmy Pens; (b) F.N. Gooptu and (c) Model Industries, Dayalbagh, Agra. F.N. Gooptu also features in a listing of makers of fountain pen clips, made of gold and nickel.

Calcutta Horn Manufacturing may be an incorrect listing, as the *All India Swadeshi Directory*, published in 1933,[40]

---

[39]*Desher Katha: Swadeshi Shilper Talika*, Swadeshi Shilpa Prachar Samiti, Bengali year 1338.
[40]*All India Swadeshi Directory*, Allahabad Law Journal Press, Allahabad, 1933.

lists the company as a maker of combs, shoe-horns and stroppers for razors. No records seem to exist for P. Ghosh and Brothers or for Orient Nibs. According to the *All India Swadeshi Directory*, Model Industries was fairly diversified, with a basket that encompassed artwork, weighing machines, buttons, cutlery, electrical goods and gramophones. But yes, it also made fountain pens. The Dayalbagh area of Agra is associated with the Radhasoami faith and was established in 1915. From 1916, there was a conscious attempt to develop small-scale industries, under the umbrella of Model Industries. Understandably, fountain pens or nibs were a small part of the portfolio of Model Industries.[41]

D.J. Dabholkar and Company, stationers, printers and general merchants, located in Poona (now Pune), does not feature in the list above. Established in 1922, it made dip pens but there is no evidence of this enterprise ever having ventured into fountain pens.

If the Bengali booklet is not completely reliable, what listing does the *All India Swadeshi Directory* have for makers of fountain pens? It includes: (a) A.M. Rasul and Sons, Lyallpur; (b) F.N. Gooptu, Calcutta; (c) Hari Singh and Company, Gunjipur, Jubbulpore; (d) Luxmy Stylo Pen Works; (e) National Fountain Pen Works, Lucknow; (f) Nagar and Company, Allahabad (now Prayagraj); (g) Prem Narayan Electrical Engineering[42], Meerut; (h) S.R. and Jivan Brothers, Jubbulpore; (i) Sarkar Brothers, Purulia; (j) Sandil Industries, Lucknow; and (k) Satya Kumar

---

[41]Model Industries Limited was incorporated in 1944 and liquidated much later.

[42]Rather unusually, Prem Narayan Electrical Engineering are described as producing capless fountain pens.

Banerjee, Calcutta. Of these, other than Luxmy pens and Gooptu pens, no records exist for any of the others.

As for nibs, we have a list of 12 'Indian' or 'Swadeshi' nib manufacturers in 1933. They were: (a) C.M. Karmakar and Company, Comilla; (b) F.N. Gooptu and Company, Calcutta; (c) Ideal Pen Works, Sialkote; (d) Ishwar Singh, Lahore; (e) Kulkarni Brothers, Bombay (now Mumbai); (f) M. Hirday Narain, Lucknow; (g) Model Industrial, Agra; (h) Nib Manufacturing Company, Bombay;[43] (i) Puri Iron Works, Gujrat, Punjab;[44] (j) Tambat Brothers, Gwalior; (k) V.S. Ball and Company, Bombay; and (l) Waise Brothers, Sialkot. These may have been nibs for dip pens, not necessarily fountain pens. The nib manufacturers mentioned by Dr Saha do feature in this list. He seems to have got the location of Tambat Brothers wrong, as the Tambat Factory was in Gwalior, not in Mumbai. The Tambat Nib Factory was important enough to be mentioned in *A Handbook of Gwalior*, published in 1936. 'Established at Kurla in 1907, the factory was shifted to Gwalior in 1911. It manufactures writing pen nibs of 18 varieties and hair and drawing pins. The machine plant (of nibs and pen manufacture) is designed and built by Tambat Brothers themselves at their own works [...] Tambat Brothers have been awarded "special appointment warrant" by His Highness the Maharaja Scindia.'[45]

It is reasonable to conjecture that these two listings are exhaustive and capture all manufacturers of fountain pens, nibs and ink till the end of the 1920s. But one still needs to

---

[43]In Sandhurst Road, Girgaon.
[44]This is Gujrat from the Punjab Province in Pakistan.
[45]Garde, M.B., *A Handbook of Gwalior*, Alijah Darbar Press, Gwalior, 1936.

be careful. Dr Saha got the first prototype for a fountain pen made by Nilmony Karmakar. What did Karmakar do before this and why did Saha choose him? Did he possess any special expertise in making or repairing pens?

Serampore (Srirampur), neighbouring Calcutta, passed from Danish to British hands in 1845 and became a centre of missionary, educational, printing and even industrial activity. The spread of education was invariably correlated with use of pens and fountain pens, which were mostly imported. These pens had to be repaired, and from repairs, it was a short step to making fountain pens. Three universities were set up in 1857, in Calcutta, Madras (now Chennai) and Bombay. A commission set up to examine the Indian education system in 1882,[46] stated in its report, 'The function of these Universities is that of examination, and not of instruction. The latter is conducted by the affiliated colleges and other institutions authorized to send up candidates for the university examinations.'[47] The structure thus established was decentralized, modelled on systems prevalent in Britain.

The University of Osmania was established in 1918, bringing teachers and students together, creating the need for writing instruments. A farmer from Allahabad, S.A. Siddiqui, identified this business opportunity. He first bought imported pens from Calcutta, especially Conway Stuart Duro Pens,[48] and started to sell them in Hyderabad, initially door-to-door and then at

---

[46]Since this was headed by William Wilson Hunter, it is usually known as the Hunter Commission.
[47]'Report of the Indian Education Commission', Superintendent of Government Printing, Calcutta, 1883.
[48]A model launched in 1924

Deccan Pen Stores, established in 1918. He then got dealerships from other foreign pen manufacturers. However, pens that had been sold would get damaged and customers would come back to get them repaired. That led to Deccan Pen Stores actually making fountain pens and selling them under its own brand name. Several years down the line, the pattern was no different for Hilal Pen Stores, also in Hyderabad. Abdul Razzaq Farooqi originally hailed from Kashmir and eventually joined the Nizam of Hyderabad's army. After retirement, he set up a pen shop in 1907 near Charminar, which became a much larger pen shop in 1932, after his death and in a different part of Hyderabad. But this still meant importing fountain pens and selling them, until Hilal Pen Stores started making its Sultan brand of pens in 1952.

This pattern was replicated in other parts of India. In the 1920s, Gem and Company was set up in Madras by S. Venkat Rangam Chetty and M.C. Cunnan. The brand, which still exists, is known as Gama.[49] The name alludes to Ghulam Mohammad Baksh Butt (1878–1960), known as the Great Gama, the world wrestling champion, who was at the height of his fame in the 1920s. There is one particular Gama model, the Gama Supreme, which is so large that it does resemble a wrestler. However, before this brand had been established, Gem and Company used to import Parker and Waterman pens and sell them in India. It was, therefore, remarkable that the first Gama pens should have been designed in Madras and made in England. As Pratap Kumar of Gama Pens says,

> We did not focus on branding value creation for Gama, instead we wanted to give the utility value to

---

[49]The trademark was registered in Tamil Nadu in 1950.

the customer: the pleasure of the feel of writing with a Gama fountain pen. If we were to focus on branding value, the price would have shot up by 10 folds [...] We had four brands: Gama, Sigma, Alpha and Beta [...] Manufacturing ED pens which do not leak in the body section and flows properly is a different cup of tea. The easy way out was a cartridge or a convertor! There are many hobby manufacturers who make pens with a converter or cartridge. They are not able to make ED pens as they are more challenging, that is where Gama Pens come into picture with traditional manufacturing and proper turning. We don't use CNC machines.[50]

BHU was established in 1916, just two years before Osmania. If Osmania University triggered a demand for writing instruments, BHU must also have had a similar effect. Therefore, in the late 1930s, Tara Prasad Sahu switched from selling fodder to selling fountain pens near the BHU campus, catering specifically to BHU students. In 1946, this became Penco, which is also a bit of a pen museum now. Penco not only dealt with foreign brands, it eventually started to sell its own brands.

At around the time, Honest Pen Hospital was established in the city of Thrissur in 1937 by Kaalathodu Koluthu Parambil Abdulla. Though not makers of fountain pens, both Kaalathodu Koluthu Parambil Abdulla and S.A. Siddiqui learnt the skills

---

[50]Ganguly, Chawm, 'Gama Pens—a pilgrimage to the shrine of Pratap Kumar, the reigning deity', Inked Happiness, 22 June 2021, https://bit.ly/3PCwQ8e. Accessed on 24 May 2022. Snippets from an interview with Pratap Kumar of Gama Pens. ED means an eye-dropper pen and CNC stands for computer numerical control.

of repairing pens from Calcutta. As the then capital of British India, it was but natural that there should be several agents in Calcutta who imported foreign pens. It was also natural that these pen-users would wish to get their pens repaired. Several pen hospitals sprouted all over Calcutta and one such pen hospital (in Esplanade) dates back to the 1920s.

As we move towards the end of the 1920s, we should ask ourselves, what exactly do we mean when we use the expression, 'maker of an Indian fountain pen'? In his book, Dr Saha referred to Luxmy Stylo Pen Works as India's first 'machine-turned fountain pen factory'. The use of that adjective tends to suggest that hand-turned fountain pen manufacturers existed, except that they were small-scale and unorganized and no records exist for them. Nilmony Karmakar may very well have had some experience of making fountain pens, perhaps by hand. Another example from Calcutta in 1907 is S.K. Das, who advertised 'ink reservoir' pens, which were, of course, nothing but fountain pens. The brand names used were Independent and Eagle. However, decades later, it is impossible to figure out when a fountain pen is really locally made and when it is imported, repackaged and rebranded. Hence, we are left with Luxmy Pens and F.N. Gooptu.

## F.N. Gooptu and Gandhi's Pen

Fanindra Nath Gooptu was born in 1878 in Calcutta, the grandson of Dr Dwaraka Nath Gooptu and the son of Gopal Chandra Gooptu. Dwaraka Nath Gooptu was not only a physician but also an entrepreneur who established his own pharmacy, D.N. Gooptu and Company.[51] The entrepreneurial streak in his grandfather brushed off on the grandson. Indeed, his father, Gopal Chandra Gooptu, wanted Gooptu to start a manufacturing business.[52] Gooptu established his own fountain pen manufacturing company more or less at the same time as Dr Saha, in 1905, when he was still in his twenties. The inspiration was partly his grandfather and the entrepreneurial experience he had gained from his grandfather's company while still in college. In the general environment of inspiration, one should also mention Kaliprosanna Ghosh (1843–1910), journalist, author, influential thinker, Rai Bahadur and Dewan. His thoughts inspired many young Bengalis to turn to entrepreneurship. Gooptu's primary motivation was driving entrepreneurship and in 1908, he also established a forum known as Bengal Initiative, for the development of Bengal.

Gooptu died in March 1935. Since these are forgotten pages, it is worth quoting from one of the obituaries for him.[53]

In pursuance of this belief he founded what has since become a vast concern, namely, Messrs. F.N. Gooptu and Company, manufacturers of pencils, pens, nibs and fountain pens... F.N. Gooptu products are now a household word and no Bengali thinks of writing materials without unconsciously associating them with the undertaking founded by the Rai Bahadur [...] He conceived the idea

[51]Dr Dwaraka Nath Gooptu established this company at the age of 22.
[52]'History of Dr D. Gooptu', Dr Dwarakanath Gooptu, 10 July 2015, https://bit.ly/3yWQ2Ym. Accessed on 24 May 2022.
[53]Ramaprosad Gooptu went abroad to study the manufacture of fountain pens. Hence, Gooptu started making fountain pens between 1925 (Mahatma Gandhi's visit) and 1935 (his death), after Dr Saha.

of starting a small manufactory of pens, pencils and nibs in the compound of his residential building at No. 5 Middleton Street, Calcutta [...] The demand for F.N. Gupta [*sic*] products increased by leaps and bounds and in 1910 it was found necessary to move the manufactory to more spacious quarters at No. 12 Beliaghata Road. The Government of Bengal had by that time extended their patronage to the products of the firm after critical examination. Ever since that time the manufactory has grown and developed until today it occupies the proud position of being the largest concern of its kind in the whole of India [...] Mahatma Gandhi during a visit to Calcutta in 1925 inspected the manufactory and bestowed the highest encomiums upon the enterprise of Fanindra Nath [...] Until now, however, Fanindra Nath had not been able to fulfil a long cherished ambition—the manufacture of fountain pens. Not many years ago he sent his son, Mr Ramaprosad Gooptu, to specialize in the art of fountain pen making [...] Today fountain pens manufactured by this firm have flooded the market and compete most successfully with the imported article.[54]

F.N. Gooptu and Company was established in Middleton Street, in the residence of Gopal Chandra Gooptu. There are suggestions that preparations for setting up the company may have started earlier, perhaps in 1901, but 1905 is usually mentioned as its foundation year, as stated in the comprehensive

[54]'Late Rai Bahadur F.N. Gooptu, A Great Industrialist,' *Landholders Journal*, Vol. 3, No. 5-8, 1935, https://bit.ly/3tThQcF. Accessed on 22 June 2022. The title of Rai Bahadur was conferred to Gooptu in 1920 in recognition of services rendered during World War I.

book on Swadeshi enterprise in Bengal between 1910 and 1920.[55] This same book has a section on pens, penholders and nibs, in a chapter under the 'miscellaneous' heading. Gooptu was interested in making pencils, penholders (that is, dip pens) and nibs, which he started doing by sourcing juniper wood from East Africa and graphite from Germany.

> The firm flourished so quickly that from 1907, the government made contracts to purchase its products. This was one of the very few instances when the government tended to express some sort of encouragement to indigenous enterprise. It is notable that unlike many other Swadesh businessmen, F.N. Gupta [sic] did not go abroad to get training in manufacture, but started making these articles by the application of his own creative talent.[56]

The switch to making fountain pens clearly occurred post-World War I, after Ramaprosad Gooptu went to England and Germany to pick up the required skills. Mahatma Gandhi's visit to the factory in 1925 made this amply clear.[57] The testimonial makes

---

[55]Bhattacharyya, Amit, *Swadeshi Enterprise in Bengal*, 1900–1920, Mita Bhattacharyya, Calcutta, 1986..

[56]Ibid.

[57]Mahatma Gandhi wrote a testimonial about his visit to Gooptu's factory in August 1925: 'It has been a great pleasure to me to be able to visit this pencil and penholder factory. I was delighted to be informed some of the machines were designed and made in this factory. I wish this national enterprise every success.' Gandhi, M.K., *Mahatma Gandhi's Collected Works*, Vol. 32, Gandhi Sevagram Ashram, https://bit.ly/3PEdwra. Accessed on 24 May 2022. A fountain pen used by Gooptu has been found, printed with the year 1925. But this seems to have been imported and not made in Calcutta. An advertisement in the Bengali monthly *Prabasi*

no mention of fountain pens. Part of the confusion has been created by what Purushottam Ganesh Mavalankar, Speaker of the Constituent Assembly and first Speaker of the Lok Sabha, wrote:

> It was May 1944. Bapu was at Juhu. I went to him with my father. After the talks (between him and my father) were over, I placed in Bapu's hands my autograph-book for his autograph. He took the book with the five rupee note, and asked for a fountain pen, which was then offered to him by my father. But he returned it, stating that it was of foreign make. He even rejected my pen, which was known as 'Gooptu's Perfection' and was made at Calcutta, under the impression that it was of foreign make. He signed his autograph with a pen lying near him. While signing his autograph, he gave us, in a romantic manner, the history of his own pen. He said: 'Once I had been to Banaras. Mahadev was with me. I lost my pen there. Mahadev was naturally upset. So our host, the late Shivaprasad Gupta, presented a pen to me. He gave one to Mahadev also. I am still using that pen. It is entirely Indian-made—manufactured in Banaras—and it works well.' After saying this, he said with a smile: 'I was told the story (of the manufacture of the pen) by Shivaprasad. I do not know anything about it. But what he stated must have been true.'[58]

has also been found, with F.N. Gooptu advertising pens, dated 1923.

[58]Mavalankar, P.G., 'Sweet And Sad', Gandhi Comes Alive, 21 November 1948, https://bit.ly/3GRVU7n. Accessed on 22 June 2022.

The book by Sovan Roy[59] establishes that this pen presented by Shivaprasad Gupta was a Saha Luxmy Pen. But we also know that Mavalankar, who would have been 16 in 1944, used Gooptu's Perfection.

The Gooptu pens were marketed under the brand name Gooptu's Perfection, with popular and elite models that had gold nibs and limited editions with a mother of pearl finish.[60] In 1958, in the report of the Ministry of Labour and Employment, Gooptu's company was listed as one of India's large industrial establishments, employing 127 workers.[61] This listing mentions the name of the company as F.N. Gupta and Company's Pencil Factory, located in Beliaghata Road, Calcutta. Indeed, the enterprise made pencils, fountain pens and nibs, which is why it was also listed as a Swadeshi nib manufacturer. But gradually, it moved away from making fountain pens. In 1965, F.N. Gooptu and Company Private Limited was incorporated, with the objective of 'trading' in pencils, pens, refills, stamps, typewriter ribbons and stationery articles. In 1971, Gooptu's Pencil Industries Private Limited was incorporated. However, today, neither company exists in the Ministry of Corporate Affairs' (MCA) database.[62] They have been struck off. What remains is a proud legacy.

---

[59]Roy, Sovan, *Radhika Nath Saha: Unsung Hero of Indian Fountain Pen*, Kabitika, 2019.

[60]Indrajit Chatterjee has a lot of information, and pictures, about Gooptu's pens on his blog: 'Gooptu Family Tree', Gooptu Fountain Pens & Pencils, https://bit.ly/3sTLyOd. Accessed on 24 May 2022.

[61]*Large Industrial Establishments in India*, Ministry of Labour and Employment, Labour Bureau, 1958.

[62]'MCA Services: Company/LLP Master Data', Ministry of Corporate Affairs, https://bit.ly/3xuD55F. Accessed on 15 June 2022.

## Swadeshi and the Fountain Pen

The establishment of Gooptu's company coincided with the Swadeshi movement in Bengal in 1905–06, fuelled partly by the aborted division of Bengal in 1905. Sumit Sarkar has published a comprehensive book on the Swadeshi movement in Bengal between 1903 and 1908 titled *The Swadeshi Movement in Bengal 1903-1908*.[63] He writes, 'The air was full of Swadeshi schemes—textile mills and improved handlooms, river transport concerns, match and soap factories, earthenware and tanneries.'[64] Of course, Swadeshi enterprise pre-dated 1903. We are not concerned with what shackled such Swadeshi enterprises, pre- and post-1908—credit problems, relative attractiveness of trade and so on. Till the end of the 1920s, in Bengal or elsewhere, it was a bit too early for fountain pens, as domestic manufacturing had not quite started. There were only Dr Saha and Gooptu. Fountain pens were typically imported—Parker, Sheaffer, Waterman, Swan, Blackbird and Pilot being the obvious brands. Importers often turned to making pens. Customers required their pens to be repaired and serviced. From this, it was a natural transition to resort to in-house manufacturing, even if small-scale. But that would occur later.

Sri Aurobindo wrote on India's possible comparative advantage in making nibs, though that does not necessarily mean nibs for fountain pens, as opposed to nibs for dip pens. Among the larger local producers, other than Tambat Brothers

---

[63]This specific timeline was determined by the announcement of the first draft of the partition plan (of Bengal in 1903) and the Maniktala arrests of 1908.

[64]Sarkar, Sumit, *The Swadeshi Movement in Bengal 1903-1908*, People's Publishing House, 1973.

and F.N. Gooptu, there were Hirday Narain and Golbadan Swadeshi Factory. There seems to be no record of what happened subsequently to the C.M. Karmakar and Company of Comilla.[65] At that time, there were other nib manufacturers in Barisal and Dhaka too, besides Comilla. Golbadan Swadeshi Factory, set up in Dhaka in 1904–05, was one of the larger ones. It produced handmade penholders, which competed quite successfully with machine-made penholders, imported from Germany and England.[66] Many companies made both pen-holders and nibs. With his focus on Bengal, Amit Bhattacharyya gives a list of these manufacturers, including: (a) Gupta and Company, Barisal; (b) Singha and Basu, Calcutta; (c) Swadeshi Bhandar, Purulia; (d) Bandhabpara Karmasamiti, Barisal; (e) Sen and Company, Comilla; (f) Lalana Mohan Roy Brothers, Faridpur; (g) Swadeshi Silpa Niketan, Calcutta; (h) S.U. and Company, Noakhali; and (i) Barisal Nib Manufactory, Barisal.

For instance, we are told that there were individual attempts to make pencils, holders and nibs. These were exhibited in local and district-level industrial fairs. But the quality left a lot to be desired.

> It has been reported that a naib of the Gouripur estate of Mymensingh, in a letter to his employer from Sunamgunj in Sylhet, wrote 'with great difficulty, with a bad, old and worn-out Swadeshi nib'. It is better not to make generalisation on the basis of this single evidence and

---

[65]Comilla is now in Bangladesh.
[66]Bhattacharyya, Amit, *Swadeshi Enterprise in Bengal, 1900-1920*, Mita Bhattacharyya, Calcutta, 1986.

describe the quality of the nibs as 'atrocious'.[67]

In 1950, a sub-committee on cottage industries for the United Provinces published a report titled 'Report of the Cottage Industry Sub-Committee'. This refers to fountain pens and to Hirday Narain, one of the larger producers of nibs.

> One of the most important industries which has recently developed is the fountain pen making industry. One Mr Hirday Narain of Lucknow was the first man to undertake the manufacture of pens and pen nibs. Dayal Bagh was the next institution which manufactured complete fountain pens. The Goel Fountain Pen Works at Kanpur has done considerable work in the manufacture of gold nibs. The factory has set up improvised machines of its own for nibs and other parts of fountain pens. This is indeed a creditable achievement. The factory claims to have produced all parts except the rubber tubes. During the war there was a great set-back in the manufacture of pens. The figure of the production of pens and pen nibs, unfortunately are not available. With the growth of literacy in the Province this industry bids to be one

---

[67]Ibid.

The apparent contradiction about quality assertions in the quote is because of the great variability. Few concerns were large-scale. Additional ones mentioned from geographical areas that are now in West Bengal were U. Ghosh (a student from Bengal National College), Ramchandra Bhattacharya and Probodh Chandra Basu (from Sarisa) and Mohim Chandra Dey (from Bankura). Although Amit Bhattacharyya doesn't mention this name, we have also found a stray mention of S.K. Das of Hatkhola.

of outstanding importance and deserving of all support and encouragement from Government.[68]

This quote and the reference to both Hirday Narain and Goel drive home that everything floating around can't be blindly accepted, even if it has been printed. This transformation in Hirday Narain came much later. In the 1920s, Hirday Narain had only begun. Nothing further can be discovered about Goel Fountain Pen Works, which was based in Kanpur. It probably never existed. From an income tax case that went up to the Supreme Court in 1970, we know that Lala Hriday Narain Goel was the head of a Hindu Undivided Family that engaged in various kinds of business.[69] Hence, Hirday Narain and Goel might refer to the same enterprise. In 1949, a partnership firm was formed under the name of Hirday Narain Yogendra Prakash, Yogendra Prakash being Hirday Narain's eldest son. Much later, in 1982, this was incorporated as Hirday Narain Yogendra Prakash Properties Private Limited. But Hirday Narain must have produced more than nibs. The aforementioned *All India Swadeshi Directory* included an advertisement for the National brand of fountain pens, made by Hirday Narain of Lucknow.

## Ink: Liquid and Solid

A company that made fountain pens also tended to make ink. The two went hand in hand. PM Bagchi and Luxmy Stylo Pen Works were makers of fountain pen ink. In this context, the

---

[68]*Report of the Cottage Industries Sub-Committee*, United Provinces, Allahabad, 1950.

[69]'Hirday Narain vs Income-Tax Officer, Bareilly on 21 July, 1970', Indian Kanoon, https://bit.ly/3LHt9e7. Accessed on 24 May 2022.

problem of trying to identify manufacturers of fountain pen ink, as opposed to those who manufactured printing ink or ink for dip pens gets highlighted. At that time, ink was not always liquid. It was also sold in the form of tablets and powders, which had to be mixed with water. 'As tablets were easily portable, these could be sent to the suburbs and rural areas.'[70] The Bengali booklet listing Swadeshi industries mentions the following as producers of fountain pen ink: (a) Kajal Kali, Canning Street, Calcutta; (b) Jyotsna, Calcutta; (c) Lasso, Calcutta; (d) Water Lily, Calcutta; (e) Eagle, Calcutta; (f) PM Bagchi, Calcutta; and (g) Sulekha-Himani, Calcutta.[71] In this list, the mention of Sulekha-Himani, distinct from the more famous Sulekha, which would come later, is particularly interesting. Amit Bhattacharyya's book mentions U.C. Chakraborty and Company, Bhattacharjee and Company, Sunrise Manufacturing Company, Peacock Ink Works, Sulav Ink Factory, Bengal Ink Factory, Bagbazar Ink Factory and Binapani Ink Store.[72] All these firms produced ink tablets. Other brands also figure among names of firms that sold ink tablets, including Red Cross (Robin Sen and Company), Scissor (Sen Ink Factory), Imperial (B.C. Chakravarty and Company), Standard (Standard Manufacturing Company) and Mayur (Paul and Company).

The 1933 *All India Swadeshi Directory* has separate listings

---

[70]Bhattacharyya, Amit, *Swadeshi Enterprise in Bengal, 1900-1920*, Mita Bhattacharyya, Calcutta, 1986.

[71]*Desher Katha: Swadeshi Shilper Talika*, Swadeshi Shilpa Prachar Samiti, Bengali year 1338.

[72]Bhattacharyya, Amit, *Swadeshi Enterprise in Bengal, 1900-1920*, Mita Bhattacharyya, Calcutta, 1986.

for printing ink, fountain pen ink and ink.[73] The last heading presumably means that other kinds of ink, besides printing or fountain pen ink, were being manufactured. The listed manufacturers for fountain pen ink were Agra Chemical and Pharmaceutical Works; Bengal Industrial Company; Chemical Association, Calcutta (the makers of Kajal Kali); Glove Ink Manufacturers, Lahore; H.D. Nariman Brothers, Bombay; Industrial Research House, Allahabad; Lunar Works, Allahabad; Model Industries, Dayalbagh; Monarch Ink Manufacturing Company, Badaun; N.K.M. Abbas, Trivandrum; National Commercial House, Lucknow; M. Hirday Narain, Lucknow; Norman's Ink, Bombay; Oriental Works, Hyderabad, Sind; Perfect Chemical Works, Lahore; Saraju, Calcutta; Saraswati Ink Works, Madras; Samar and Brothers, Calcutta; Varma and Brothers, Madras; Vishnu Industrial Works, Baroda; and Waterlily Chemical Works, Calcutta. This list also highlights geographical areas where industrialization spread. Fountain pen and ink manufacturing mirrored general industrial development.

One should not automatically assume that this listing is complete and accurate. For instance, it is known that Krishnaveni Inks in Madras started making ink from 1920. Strictly speaking, the name of the enterprise was Krishnaveni Ink Factory and it was Sambasiva Rao's proprietary concern, until his death in 1977. A 1945 trademark application mentioned Krishnaveni as a trademark for not only writing ink and fountain pen ink, but also ink powders and tablets.[74] The point is that there is

---

[73]*All India Swadeshi Directory,* Allahabad Law Journal Press, Allahabad, 1933.
[74]In 1971, an additional trademark application was filed for 'Kriveni Ink'.

no mention of Krishnaveni under the heading of makers of fountain pen ink. However, the listing under the 'ink' heading does mention Krishnavari Ink Works, Madras. This probably leads to a double deduction. First, intellectual property rights, like trademarks, were not regarded as very important. Second, the mindset was still, even as late as 1945, one of ink powder and tablets, not liquid ink.

An advertisement in the Directory, by Mohan and Sons, from Lucknow, captures the flavour of the times.

> Manufacturer of Swadeshi Writing Inks, such as Ordinary Blue Black ink, Red ink, Black ink for *khatta*s, Red ink of superior quality and Blue Black ink of superior quality which writes a clear blue and gradually changes to an intense black, Fountain pen ink, it flows easily and smoothly from the pen and retains its remarkable fluidity under exposure which can be used in any kind of Fountain Pens, and Blue Black and Red inks Powders specially prepared from chemicals which is easily soluble either in cold or in hot water, which can be used at once without straining, and produces a superfine writing ink and Rubber stamping inks voilet [*sic*] and green colours. [75]

The story of Kajal Kali (Chemical Association), one of the larger producers of fountain pen ink, is best expressed in the words of Chawm Ganguly.[76]

---

[75] *All India Swadeshi Directory*, Allahabad Law Journal Press, Allahabad, 1933.

[76] Ganguly, Chawm, 'Fountain Pen & Ink—the Calcutta connection,' Inked Happiness, 13 September 2020, https://bit.ly/3yUwEex. Accessed on 24 May 2022.

It would be decades later, in 1924 to be precise, that three enterprising students from Shantiniketan—Hiten Nandi, Tarun Roy and Sisir Sen would get into the manufacture of inks, establishing Kajal Kali, that had the blessings of none other than the poet laureate Rabindra Nath Tagore, who is known to have expressed his satisfaction having used the ink and had gone on record to state that the dark sheen of Kajal was no less than those of imported inks. As a matter of fact, many experts are of the opinion that this was the first commercial effort to produce writing ink as we know it, in Bengal. That Kajal Kali was immensely successful is unequivocal. It will not be fair, however, if we do not mention the fact that in the same year Krishnabeni inks were also started in Madras. It is also a fact that even Luxmy had its own ink which was commercially available much before Kajal Kali was made. The story of Swadeshi Fountain Pen & Ink is indeed full of such interesting turns.[77]

---

[77]Since Kajal Kali was often advertised as the first producer of fountain pen ink, it is possible that that this was a reference to the process or the dye, as compared to preceding attempts by the likes of PM Bagchi. When using the expression 'decades later', Chawm Ganguly is referring to PM Bagchi. The original letter by Rabindranath Tagore, dated 27 February 1930, is in Apurba Kumar Panda's collection. Kajal Kali's staple was permanent blue black ink. In Bengali, the word 'kalima' means blackness and it is impossible to translate the entire nuance of the way Tagore used the word in his letter of appreciation. However, Chawm Ganguly conveys the sense pretty well.

# 3

## GANDHI AND AMBEDKAR

Limited edition fountain pens can be expensive and are never an average indicator of fountain pens or fountain pen markets. There are different lists of the most expensive pens in the world in which the dividing line between a fountain pen and an item of jewellery gets blurred. But across lists, among manufacturers of the most expensive fountain pens in the world, Montblanc will find its place, along with Caran d'Ache and Aurora. Indeed, the average Montblanc fountain pen is expensive, limited editions more than others. Not long ago, there was a controversy over Montblanc's limited-edition Gandhi pen for linking luxury pens with the name of a man who stood for the poor and fought against poverty. A court case was filed regarding this issue in the Kerala High Court. There were two limited-edition pens actually—silver and gold—a Limited Edition 3000, with three thousand fountain pens, and a Limited Edition 241 (named after the 241 miles of Gandhi's Salt March) with 241 fountain pens. Both sets had an image of Mahatma Gandhi on the nib. Apart from the violation of the Emblems and Names (Prevention of Improper Use) Act of 1950, which restricts use of the name or pictorial representation of Mahatma Gandhi, it was a bad idea to link Gandhiji's name with pens that cost several lakhs of rupees. There has been no controversy when the Aditya Birla group started to sell Eternal Gandhi products, including fountain pens. The reason is obvious—Eternal Gandhi fountain pens aren't frightfully expensive.

It isn't just a question of price. There is an element of incongruity in linking Gandhiji's name with fountain pens, regardless of price. Mahatma Gandhi didn't like fountain pens— he preferred reed pens, which were in use before the advent of fountain pens. By reed pen, he meant what is usually known as a dip pen, not a classic reed pen made from reeds. This comes across clearly in several of his letters. On 20 March 1932, he wrote to Parasram Mehrotra, 'There is not the slightest need for the girls to use a fountain pen. Really speaking, nobody in the Ashram should need a fountain pen. Why should anybody be in such hurry? For students at any rate, it is certainly a harmful thing to use. The reed-pen is the best for writing Gujarati, Hindi, Urdu and other Indian scripts.'[78] On 13 May 1932, he wrote to Mirabehn, 'It is well if you do without the fountain pen.'[79] On 17 April 1937, he wrote to Amrit Kaur, 'If we are to re-introduce village articles after being used to the Western style, we shall have to be patient and inventive. That the pen requires constant dipping is a good point. It lessens fatigue. That the fountain-pen saves time is not an unmixed blessing. The village pen and ink undoubtedly admit of improvement. That can only come when you and I use these things.'[80] In October

---

[78]Gandhi, M.K., *Mahatma Gandhi's Collected Works*, Vol. 55, Gandhi Sevagram Ashram, https://bit.ly/3msVGd9. Accessed on 9 June 2022.
[79]Ibid.
[80]Gandhi, M.K., *Mahatma Gandhi's Collected Works*, Vol. 71, Gandhi Sevagram Ashram, https://bit.ly/3tk29v1. Accessed on 9 June 2022.

1938, he wrote to Lilavati Asar, 'And do not follow Mahadev's example of writing with a fountain-pen. I tolerate Mahadev's fountain-pen because Mahadev is a scribe. You are not a scribe and are not going to be one. So, I shall not, and I should not tolerate the fountain-pen in your case.'[81] On 28 April 1947, in his 'Advice to Students', he wrote,

For example, (1) when you get up in the morning you can roll up your own bedding; (2) help in preparing your breakfast and milk, etc., whatever you take, without waiting for your mother or anyone else to prepare it and serve you; (3) give a helping hand in sweeping and scrubbing; (4) do your own laundering; (5) help your mother with the cooking and cleaning the dishes; (6) make your own cloth by spinning regularly every day; (7) keep your books clean and neatly arranged, economize on exercise books as much as possible; (8) learn to do with a pen-holder and ink costing two annas, instead of a fountain-pen costing Rs. 50.[82]

On 14 July 1947, in a letter to a child, he wrote,

You should give up your fondness for writing with a pencil or fountain-pen. Anybody who wishes to improve his handwriting should use a reed-pen. How can all the children in the country afford to use fountain-pens? I suppose you know how much a fountain-pen costs. If I was a teacher and had my way, I would forbid the bringing of

---

[81]Gandhi, M.K., *Mahatma Gandhi's Collected Works*, Vol. 74, Gandhi Sevagram Ashram, https://bit.ly/3zriJwU. Accessed on 9 June 2022.
[82]Gandhi, M.K., *Mahatma Gandhi's Collected Works*, Vol. 94, Gandhi Sevagram Ashram, https://bit.ly/3xxI6LX. Accessed on 9 June 2022.

a fountain-pen into the classroom. But mine has become a lone voice now. If you have any influence with your friends, popularize the use of the reed-pen among them. [83]

## The Reed Pen and the Village Economy

Why was Mahatma Gandhi against fountain pens? The reason had to do with his ideal of a self-sufficient village economy. In November 1934, in an article on village industries, he wrote,

> In a nutshell, of the things we use, we should restrict our purchases to the articles which villages manufacture. Their manufactures may be crude. We must try to induce them to improve their workmanship, and not dismiss them because foreign articles or even articles produced in cities, that is, big factories, are superior [...] If this is the correct attitude, then, naturally, we begin with ourselves and thus use, say, handmade paper instead of mill-made, use village reed, wherever possible, instead of the fountain pen or the penholder, ink made in the villages instead of the big factories, etc. I can multiply instances of this nature. There is hardly anything of daily use in the home which the villagers have not made before and cannot make even now. [84]

In 1937, Mahadev Desai received a letter from Prabhudas Gandhi, which said,

---

[83]Gandhi, M.K., *Mahatma Gandhi's Collected Works*, Vol. 96, Gandhi Sevagram Ashram, https://bit.ly/3msnoqA. Accessed on 9 June 2022.
[84]Gandhi, M.K., 'Chapter-4: Rehabilitation of Village Industries | Village Industries', Gandhi Sevagram Ashram, https://bit.ly/3aTyfYh. Accessed on 9 June 2022.

Some time back in an article entitled 'Wanted Rural-mindedness', you recommended, as a step in that direction, the adoption of the reed-pen in the place of the fountain-pen. I was struck by your argument, and after reading Bapu's interpretation of the A.I.V.I.A. membership pledge, I laid aside my fountain-pen and took to the reed, nine months back. I was not altogether unused to the reed-pen [...] After a month of baffling experience, however, I was again forced to return to the fountain-pen a sadder and a wiser man. The reasons which compelled the change were as follows: (1) It took three hours to copy out matter, using a reed-pen, that could be done with the fountain-pen in one hour and a half [...] (2) It took at least from a quarter of an hour to three quarters of an hour to mend one reed-pen by means of an indigenous village knife [...] (3) The fountain-pen enables you to make short jottings and entries, so indispensable in the course of village work, while standing, or while you are on the move. When I reverted to the use of the reed-pen, I invariably found that my diary-writing and maintenance of other daily records and registers fell heavily into arrears [...] Surely, it is no part of the policy of the A.I.V.I.A. to slave-drive its workers to the very limit of their capacity.[85]

Gandhiji responded through an essay titled 'The Reed versus the Fountain Pen' and said,

---

[85]Gandhi, M.K., *Mahatma Gandhi's Collected Works*, Vol. 71, Gandhi Sevagram Ashram, https://bit.ly/3tk29v1. Accessed on 9 June 2022. AIVIA stands for the All India Village Industries Association.

The village-dweller has not to work under high pressure or to speed about from place to place in motor cars and trams like the city dwellers. All this work is done by the easier and more natural modes of locomotion. Similarly the fountain-pen can have no place in his economy. I might, perhaps, reluctantly go so far as to admit the steel nib as a compromise, but that is all. The steel nib in my opinion has spelt the death of the calligraphist's art the mending of a reed-pen was itself an art. It called into play the artistic skill and the personality of the scribe that was reflected in the characters which he traced. All that has gone with the advent of the steel pen. But the steel pen has not done even half the mischief that the fountain-pen is doing. The introduction of the fountain-pen in the village, to me, marks the beginning of the end of the existence of the village as such and its slow metamorphosis into the city.[86]

This idea figured again in Gandhiji's discussion with Maurice Frydman in January 1939.

Again, I dislike fountain-pens, but just now I am making use of one though I carry a reed pen about in my box. Every time I use the fountain-pen it hurts me and I think of the neglected reed pen in my box. Compromise comes in at every step, but one must realize that it is a compromise and keep the final goal constantly in front of the mind's eye. [87]

---

[86]Ibid.

[87]Gandhi, M.K., *Mahatma Gandhi's Collected Works,* Vol. 74, Gandhi Sevagram Ashram, https://bit.ly/3zriJwU. Accessed on 9 June 2022.

It was not entirely about the self-sufficient village economy though. There was a touch of Swadeshi to this idea as well. Pens—fountain pens or reed pens—require ink. On 15 December 1932, Gandhiji wrote to Jamnalal Bajaj, 'Shri Kateli knew that we had a stock of the Swadeshi ink for fountain pen which you wanted, and, therefore, we have sent a bottle of it for you. We have quite a large quantity of it.'[88] In 1947, while advising students, he talked about fountain pens priced at 50 rupees. Though we don't have official price indices that go as far back as 1947, in today's prices, he was talking about fountain pens with price tags of roughly around 15,000 rupees. These were imported pens and they were expensive. Therefore, they were valuable enough to be donated. Thus, fountain pens figure in Gandhiji's 1934 notes on Bihar. 'At these meetings women have given their bracelets and men their rings, young students their fountain pens because they had nothing else to give.'[89] In 1937, when Gandhiji asked for donations for the Harijan Institute, *The Hindu* newspaper reported: 'Small cash, jewels, watches and fountain pens were offered.'[90]

---

[88]Gandhi, M.K., *Mahatma Gandhi's Collected Works*, Vol. 58, Gandhi Sevagram Ashram, https://bit.ly/3xxPk2J. Accessed on 9 June 2022.

[89]Gandhi, M.K., *Mahatma Gandhi's Collected Works*, Vol. 63, Gandhi Sevagram Ashram, https://bit.ly/3n6vfdF. Accessed on 22 June 2022.

[90]Reported as a note to Gandhiji's speech in Kodambakkam. Gandhi, M.K., *Mahatma Gandhi's Collected Works*, Vol. 70, Gandhi Sevagram Ashram, https://bit.ly/3xJjBKI. Accessed on 22 June 2022.

## Gandhi's Ratnam Pen

Despite his disapproval, Gandhiji did possess at least one fountain pen. On 16 July 1935, he wrote a letter to K.V. Ratnam of Ratnam Fountain Pen Works, Rajahmundry. The letter said, 'Dear Ratnam, I must thank you for the fountain pen you have sent me through Shri Kumarappa. I have received it and it seems to be a good substitute for the foreign pens one sees in the bazaars.'[91] In 1921, Kosuri Venkata Ratnam met Gandhiji in Wardha. He belonged to a family of goldsmiths, and he presented Gandhiji with some artwork. Gandhiji suggested they should manufacture products that were not too expensive and could be used by Indians. Venkata Ratnam and his brother, Satyanarayana, turned to fountain pens and set up Ratnam Pen Works in 1932.[92] Their first pen, manufactured in 1932, went to the politician and social activist Nyapathi Subba Rao Pantulu. Born in 1856, Pantulu might not have used the first fountain pen produced in India much. The second

---

[91]Gandhi, M.K., *Mahatma Gandhi's Collected Works*, Vol. 67, Gandhi Sevagram Ashram, https://bit.ly/3Oc4ArV. Accessed on 22 June 2022.

[92]Ratnam Pen Works still exists and manufactures fountain pens. Since the two brothers divided their businesses later, there is now a Ratnam Pen Works and a distinct Ratnam Ball Pen Works (which also sells fountain pens under the brand name Ratnamson). When President Ram Nath Kovind visited the Pablo Neruda Museum in Santiago on 31 March 2019, the press release by Rashtrapati Bhavan stated, 'He gifted a special pen to the Museum made by the family whom Gandhiji encouraged to develop the first indigenous fountain pen in India.' Ratnam 302, which is still produced, is the pen that had been given to Gandhiji. Ratnam pens have been gifted to other dignitaries too. For example, Prime Minister Narendra Modi gave German Chancellor Angela Merkel a Ratnam pen.

pen, made of ebonite, was sent to Mahatma Gandhi, probably in 1932, though the year might also have been 1933. Since it was not Swadeshi enough, Gandhiji rejected it. In 1935, a second pen was sent to him through J.C. Kumarappa, the then secretary of AIVIA. This pen was the subject of the 1935 letter and, evidently, Gandhiji used this Ratnam pen to write several letters.[93]

Here are parts of the Ratnam story, as recounted by Chawm Ganguly:[94] In Rajahmundry, Kosuri Erayacharya had two sons, Kosuri Venkata Ratnam (K.V. Ratnam) and Kosuri Venkata Brahmam (K.V. Brahmam). These two brothers were influenced by Mahatma Gandhi's views and wished to set up a Swadeshi fountain pen factory. However, the two brothers didn't know much about making fountain pens. According to the story, a local judge gave them a book on making fountain pens. That is how the Swadeshi fountain pen, made by hand on the basis of instructions in a book, originated. In this way, K.V. Ratnam established Ratnam Pens in Rajahmundry in 1932. He didn't monopolize the knowledge and freely shared it, allowing others to make hand-turned fountain pens. Ratnam's cousin established Brahmam in Bhimavaram. Brahmam pens are

---

[93]This account is based on the following sources: Samson, Raj, 'Ratnam & Sons: Penning a Legacy,' The Hans India, 18 November 2016, https://bit.ly/39Xo5p2. Accessed on 25 May 2022; Doval, Nikita, 'To Pen the Swadeshi Narrative,' Open, 27 September 2019, https://bit.ly/3NBruIE. Accessed on 25 May 2022; Amin, Tushar A., 'India-Made Fountain Pens Thrive on Global Demand,' Money Control, 17 October 2013, https://bit.ly/3wQhc0r. Accessed on 25 May 2022.

[94]Ganguly, Chawm, 'Ratnam Son—for, the name is the fame!' Inked Happiness, 22 June 2019, https://bit.ly/3NBvYiM. Accessed on 9 June 2022.

difficult to get now and are a collector's delight. The business grew and the two brothers divided it up. One of Ratnam's sons stuck to making fountain pens as K.V. Ratnam and Sons. But Kosuri Venkata Narasimha Chary, Ratnam's eldest son, went to Germany and learnt how to make ballpoint pens, establishing Ratnam Ball Pen Works in 1958.

One of Gandhiji's pens was stolen, though there is nothing to indicate this was the Ratnam pen. It probably was not, since the stolen pen had been an expensive one. 'Most people have lost a pen at some time or the other. So did Gandhi. He had a costly fountain pen which was pilfered. The pen was immediately replaced but the theft pained him. Henceforth, he decided, he would not use anything so attractive that it would tempt someone to steal it. He began using a pen-holder and a nib.'[95] Mirabehn also referred to the incident of the fountain pen being stolen.

It is not a fountain pen which he is using; some misfortune happened to his last one, since when he writes with an ordinary nib and holder. The ink-pot is one of Bapu's little patents, and consists of a tiny balm bottle fixed in a wooden stand which also carries pen and pencils. The little old tin screw top of the balm bottle Bapu most delicately puts off and on every time he uses his 'ink-stand.'[96]

[95]"Chapter 7: Basic Pen | Short Stories for Everyone, Inspiring incidents from Gandhiji's Life: Selected from the book Everyone's Gandhi', Gandhi Sevagram Ashram, https://bit.ly/398fNuk. Accessed on 9 June 2022.
[96]Mirabehn, 'His Daily Life', Gandhi Comes Alive, Mani Bhavan Gandhi Sangrahalaya, 24 January 1948, https://bit.ly/3xue2AV. Accessed on 9 June 2022.

Occasionally, Mahatma Gandhi did use fountain pens. There are photographs of him doing so. For instance, there is a 1940 photograph of Gandhiji taken by Kanu Gandhi, reproduced quite often. It has Gandhiji seated, writing with a fountain pen. In 2018, a rare photograph of Gandhiji was auctioned, depicting him walking with Madan Mohan Malaviya at the time of the Round Table Conference in 1931. This rare photograph was signed by Mahatma Gandhi with a fountain pen.

## Ambedkar's Fondness for Fountain Pens

The Poona Pact was signed on 24 September 1932 and Dr Rajendra Prasad, Babasaheb Ambedkar and C. Rajagopalachari were its signatories. It is said that, 'While signing the pact, Rajagopalachari was so much [*sic*] overjoyed that he exchanged his fountain-pen with Dr. Ambedkar.'[97] It would have been quite something had Ambedkar exchanged his pen with Mahatma Gandhi's pen.

Ambedkar was fond of fountain pens, not reed pens.

Apart from books, he had an insatiable desire to possess fountain pens and outsize ones at that! No ordinary ones would do, and John, who attended to his pen and stationery needs, used always to scamper and collect all the outsize pens available in town and offer them to him, one by one. The Doctor would lean heavily against a show-case and try pen after pen on a writing pad, scrawling

[97]Narake, Hari, et al. (eds.), *Dr. Babasaheb Ambedkar: Writings and Speeches*, Vol. 17 (Part-I), Ministry of Social Justice and Empowerment, Government of India, 2003, https://bit.ly/3mrjuOR. Accessed on 9 June 2022.

his broad sprawling autograph on its pages. At the end of these trials, he would grab half a dozen pens that he fancied and thrust them into his capacious coat pocket![98]

Babasaheb Ambedkar was especially fond of Parker, Sheaffer and Waterman pens. In Bombay, his fountain pens (and other stationery) came from Thacker and Company. In Delhi, they came from Dhoomimal Dharamdas (now the Dhoomimal Gallery). Portraits, pictures and statues of Ambedkar often show him with a fountain pen in his hand or pocket—a symbol of modernity. Gandhiji is depicted with his reed pen. The exchange of the reed pen for the fountain pen is part of India's economic transition and is reflected in the attitudes of these two great leaders—Gandhi and Ambedkar.

---

[98]Rao, U.R., 'I Rewrote the Blurb of His "Pakistan"', in, Yusufji, Salim (ed.), *Ambedkar: The Attendant Details*, Navayana, 2017. In this quote, 'John' refers to John Thacker.

# 4

## IMPORTS AND SWADESHI: THE ROARING 1930s AND 1940s

In the 1930s and 1940s, leading up to Independence and immediately after it, Swadeshi and imported products coexisted. Swadeshi did not necessarily mean large-scale, a point we have made before. Nor did large-scale necessarily mean an incorporated firm. Indeed, till the end of the 1940s, the MCA database mentions only five companies that are linked to pens—India Pen and Allied Industries Limited (1944), Hindustan Pen Manufacturing Company (1946), Pen Service Agency Limited (1947), Donic Pen Company Limited (1949) and Wilson Pen Private Limited (1949).

### The Incorporated List

India Pen and Allied Industries was set up in Calcutta in 1944. Oddly, no one has written anything about it, at least in connection with fountain pens, though the company still exists. One can only deduce that it moved away from making fountain pens a long time ago. Indeed, the company's recent portfolio is machinery and equipment. Manufacturing pencil sharpeners is the closest they get to writing instruments now. The Hindustan

Pen Manufacturing Company, which was incorporated in Mumbai in 1946, and has been dissolved now, also did not seem to have produced anything particularly significant, at least as far as writing instruments were concerned. The Donic Pen Company Limited was incorporated in Bangalore in 1949 and has also been dissolved. In 1943, Peter Thomas Noronha obtained a device trademark for the brand name Doric, and this was applicable to fountain pens, fountain pen ink and nibs.[99] The proprietor's address was given as Bandra, Bombay. Perhaps that was the reason for the one incorporated in Bangalore being called 'Donic' and not 'Doric'. Naturally, these Doric pens should not be confused with the famous Wahl Eversharp Doric pen, introduced in 1931 and retired in 1941.[100] However, one can guess why Noronha wished to trademark Doric.

While some tried to make pens, others imported pens and sold them, just as they had in the preceding decades. So far as imported pens were concerned, understandably, there was a proclivity towards British brands—Mentmore and the subsequent Platignum, Conway Stewart, Mabie Todd/Swan, Onoto and Burnham. Advertisements can be found for Joseph Gillott's too, probably establishing that dip pens had not yet completely exited. Waverley Cameron is probably better known for its nibs but they did make fountain pens too.[101] These pens

---

[99]'MCA Services: Company/LLP Master Data', Ministry of Corporate Affairs, https://bit.ly/3xuD55F. Accessed on 15 June 2022.
[100]The American brand of writing instruments, established in 1913, was originally called Eversharp. In 1916, it became Wahl Eversharp and has now been acquired by the Parker Pen Company.
[101]Waverley got its name from Sir Walter Scott's *Waverley* novels. Waverley Cameron advertisements said, 'They come as a boon and a blessing to men, the Pickwick, the Owl and the Waverley Pen.' Waverley Cameron was originally known as Macniven and Cameron Limited.

were also sold in India under various brand names, not just Pickwick, Owl, Phaeton, Nile and Commercial but under the odd name of Hindoo too. Originally, these were the names of nibs for dip pens, but the brands were carried over into fountain pens. Evidently, the Hindoo nib and fountain pen catered successfully to the niche market of British civil servants working in India. If you sold a pen, especially as an agent, it was expected you would service the pen and repair it, should the need arise. In 1947, the Pen Service Agency was set up in Calcutta to do precisely that—service pens. The company still exists, providing services of renting and leasing in Calcutta. As with many other historical fountain pen manufacturers, life has moved on. While Pen Service Agency was not remarkable, what is remarkable, given the times, is that it was incorporated.

The final manufacturer on the incorporated list was Wilson Pen Private Limited, which was established in 1949. The Wilson story is the story of the Sanghvi brothers—Dwarkadas Jivanlal Sanghvi and Vallabhdass Jivanlal Sanghvi. After a stint in Rangoon (now Yangon), where they sold pens, buying them from wholesalers, and in Calcutta (they moved there in 1941), the brothers moved to Bombay and started making parts for pens. In Calcutta, the firm was called Kiron and Company, after the name of Dwarkadas Sanghvi's son. His son's name was actually Kiran, but the Bengali signboard painter, following customary Bengali pronunciation, spelt it as 'Kiron', and Kiron it remained. Immediately after Independence, violence and unrest in Calcutta persuaded the Sanghvi brothers to move to Valsad and then to Bombay. Kiron and Company was registered as a company in 1947. Their factory in Dadar West manufactured everything except nibs. Meanwhile, Vallabhdass Sanghvi set up Dhiraj Pen Manufacturing Company in Bombay in 1947. As with

Kiron and Kiran, there was a mix-up in the naming of nibs.[102]

> In the beginning, the Nibs were imported from USA, under the brand names of Sita and Sity. However, as an error the supplier sent them a box of Nibs called Wilson instead. The war was a huge obstacle to sending the consignment back so they had no choice but to start making the pens with the un-returnable nibs. With the entire pen rebranded as Wilson, the pen sold far better than they expected and yet again another mistaken name was retained.
>
> By the mid-1940s the business grew and they had begun manufacturing all pens from scratch. The Manufacturing units moved to Andheri East and to Chakala. And they also introduced other brands such as the President. With almost a 1200 people as staff, there were people from almost all communities working together. A lot of women were hired for the first time. While the machines were worked by men, all the assembling of the pen was done entirely by women. Their daily salary at the time was around Rs. 3 to 4 per day.[103]

Both Kiron and Company and Dhiraj Pen Manufacturing Company produced Wilson pens. Eventually, Wilson Pen Private Limited was registered in 1949. Later, the Wilson trademark was registered to Kiron and Company while Dhiraj Pen Manufacturing Company introduced and registered the

---

[102]All the anecdotes from this paragraph have been sourced from: Sanghvi, Purvi, 'My Family Made the Pen that Wrote the Constitution of India', Indian Memory Project, https://bit.ly/3NRDSo3. Accessed on 25 May 2022. The other mistaken name referred to in the quote is 'Kiron' versus 'Kiran'.
[103]Ibid.

brand/trademark President.[104] There were other brands too. For instance, Kiron and Company introduced the brands Olympic and Dipco. Wilson pens were extremely popular and it is often stated that a Wilson pen was used to write the Constitution, as in the title of Purvi Sanghvi's piece cited earlier. The first draft of the Constitution was a work of calligraphy, whose borders were designed by Nandalal Bose and his students. The actual Constitution was written by Prem Behari Narain Raizada (Saxena), who came from a family of calligraphers. In the process, he used 432 nibs of the No. 303 variety.[105] Therefore, that draft of the Constitution was not written with a fountain pen. A dip pen was used instead. The Wilson pen was used by Ambedkar to write the draft of the draft, before it was handed over to Raizada. It is no longer possible to ascertain what happened to Ambedkar's Wilson pen.[106]

## New Materials and Manufacture

If we have suggested that the 1930s and 1940s roared, relatively speaking, that was not only because of incorporated enterprises. The material used to make fountain pens changed and so did methods of manufacture.

Ebonite is hard rubber, made by vulcanizing natural rubber. This technology was accidentally invented by Charles Goodyear

---

[104]These were not just for pens, but also for pencils, nibs and ink.

[105]That is, a Gillott 303, which was used a lot for copperplate calligraphy. Nib numbers are not standardized and vary from company to company.

[106]Prasad, Pallavi, 'Sifting Through History Looking for Ambedkar's "Constitution" Pen', The Quint, 24 January 2017, https://bit.ly/3PEbszn. Accessed on 25 May 2022.

in 1839, though the first patent for it was granted in 1844. In the context of fountain pens, most people use the word 'ebonite' as a generic term. Strictly speaking, ebonite is used as a brand name because the material resembles ebony—the wood. Bowling balls used to be made out of hard wood, until there was a switch to hard rubber in 1905. This included ebonite, and what was good for a bowling ball was also good for a fountain pen. Up to a point, all fountain pens were made out of ebonite and many Indian pens continue to be made of ebonite. That is a limited USP, unless one is especially fond of ebonite. Ebonite is smelly and its colours are not as attractive. There are no colours at all in BHR (black hard rubber) ebonite, though there can be engraved patterns on CBHR (chased black hard rubber) ebonite. One can chisel ebonite or coat it with metal. At a certain point in the evolution of technology, fountain pens made of ebonite were indeed superior to those made out of metals. However, ebonite is brittle. Therefore, after some experimentation with Galalith, the body of a pen started being made from celluloid, which made for colourful pens. Eventually, celluloid would be replaced by plastic resins (like acrylic), which made for even more attractive bodies.

Fountain pen connoisseurs will hotly debate the superiority of an ebonite feed versus a plastic feed. Stated simply, the capillary action is better with an ebonite feed. However, an ebonite feed cannot be injection moulded, unlike a plastic feed. An ebonite feed is made by hand, which can make it finer than any plastic feed, but this becomes a time-consuming process, and it is impossible to generate volume. The per unit cost of making a plastic feed will be lower than the per unit cost of making an ebonite feed. However, the ebonite feed, made by hand, will have much greater variability than a plastic feed, raising questions about consistency and quality. The economics works in favour of plastic feeds. But injection moulding machinery requires substantial fixed investments. The feed of a fountain pen is the bit that connects the nib with the reservoir of ink. While many fountain pen users may still prefer an ebonite feed, this will not necessarily be true of the body of the pen.

Beginning in the 1920s, what changed in the 1930s and 1940s was the manufacturing process of injection moulding, which involves injecting molten material into a mould. The material for the body, which includes the barrel and the cap, switched to celluloid and, more generally, other forms of plastic. For instance, Gooptu pens were made through an injection moulding process and so were Wilson pens. These new entrants that used injection moulding technology were concentrated in certain specific geographic areas—Calcutta, Bombay, Benares, Madras, Hyderabad and Rajahmundry. The following is a list of fountain pen makers, segregated geographically into the areas where their businesses were concentrated.

## Calcutta

1. Das Boral and Company—famous for the Lekhani brand—manufactured fountain pens and nibs, starting in the 1930s and continued till the end of the 1950s. An advertisement tells us that in 1947, a Lekhani fountain pen cost six rupees. The National Gandhi Museum possesses a Lekhani fountain pen, handmade out of ivory, presented to Gandhiji by Das Boral and Company.[107]

---

[107] The inscription on this pen (in Bengali) states, 'Das Boral and Company, Bangladesh'. The National Gandhi Museum also possesses a Parker fountain pen, gifted to Gandhiji by Jawaharlal Nehru in December 1946.

2. G.C. Law and Company (G.C. Laha in Bengali) was originally in the paints and pencil business in the 1890s and diversified into stationery products in the first decade of the twentieth century. Such was Gooptu's success that other possible entrants, like Law, were drawn to manufacturing fountain pens and ink. One such businessperson was A.P. Seal, who entered the business of pen-making in Maniktala in 1931 with his friend B.C. Dutta and with financial help from his father-in-law, G.C. Law. The key man behind this show was an ex-Gooptu mechanic, Probodh Mistri, who had, by 1932 made the first pen in the new premises. On February 23rd, 1933, none other than Rabindra Nath Tagore unveiled G.C. Law's pen commercially, and named it "Bharati". [108] G.C. Law pens were exported to Burma (now Myanmar), Ceylon (now Sri Lanka), East Asia, the Middle East and Australia. Notwithstanding this quote, there is no convincing evidence that Tagore actually named the pen Bharati.

3. In the closing decade of the nineteenth century and the early twentieth century, Dhar Brothers used to sell stationery items and razors, branded Ruby. In the 1920s, they started importing fountain pens, which they sold and repaired. Advertisements show that they imported and sold Parker (Duofold), Waterman, Swann and Blackbird pens. In the 1930s and 1940s, the firm also sourced handmade ebonite fountain pens, which were then sold under the brand name Ruby. The Ruby trademark was registered in 1952. In addition to Ruby, there were brands like Safety

---

[108]Ganguly, Chawm, 'Fountain Pen & Ink—The Calcutta Connection', Inked Happiness, 13 September 2020, https://bit.ly/3yUwEex. Accessed on 24 May 2022.

and Regular. Hence, the business was a combination of selling and repairing imported fountain pens and selling indigenized brands.

4. Ever Ready Stores sold fountain pens under the brand name, Satisfaction. These were probably imported pens, stamped with a local brand.

5. The Star brand, sold by College Stores, was probably similarly selling imported pens stamped with a local brand name.

6. The Swaraj brand of fountain pens, imported and branded by Sharma Brothers, was also similarly sourced.

7. Sulekha was famous for inks but also sold fountain pens.

8. In the early 1940s, a brand named Stemps, derived from Steel and Metal Products Limited, was quite popular. However, it was restricted to fountain pen nibs, not fountain pens.

## Bombay

1. We have already mentioned Kiron and Company and Dhiraj Pen Manufacturing Company but there were other pen-makers from Bombay too.

2. Wimco Pen Company reportedly sold the Radius brand of fountain pens. This was an Italian brand, manufactured in Turin since 1934. It is a bit strange that Wimco should sell an imported Italian fountain pen since there was no demand for Italian fountain pens at the time. However, there is no robust evidence of Wimco Pen Company having actually manufactured a local Radius brand, as opposed to a brand named Solede, which it actually sold.[109]

---

[109]Much later, in 1987, S.S.B. Metal Works was set up, dealing primarily in plastics. It also started manufacturing pens from Goregaon, Mumbai. It was trademarked in 2001 as Radius. This enterprise is in the business of manufacturing and exporting metal and plastic writing instruments of other kinds, but not fountain pens.

3.  National Pen and Plastic Industries sold pens under the Perla and National brands. A partnership firm, it eventually merged with Flair Writing Instruments. As we shall see, both Wimco Pen Company and National Pen and Plastic Industries have a common successor in Flair.

## Benares

We have already mentioned the establishment of BHU in 1916 and the fillip it gave to the demand for writing instruments. Therefore, Tara Prasad Sahu, the son of a cattle-farmer, switched to selling fountain pens and repairing them. This was the second half of the 1930s. Initially, these were imported fountain pens. However, in 1946, with the help of a master craftsman named Bhairon Prasad Vishwakarma, he also started manufacturing pens and selling them under the brand names of Penco and Ebonite.[110] Penco still exists as a pen shop, but no longer manufactures its own brand. As Benares has modernized and been renovated, so has Penco. It is a bit of a pen museum too now, with rare models of Parker, Swan, Plato, Mont Blanc, Waterman, Sheaffer and Wearever. It also has an Eversharp pen with a gold nib, known as the Tagore nib. A Tagore nib is an adjustable nib, varying from flexible to firm, which is useful for sketching and calligraphy work.

Tagore was fond of fountain pens. He possessed a similar Eversharp pen with an adjustable nib. One such fountain pen is displayed in the Rabindra Bhavan Museum in Shantiniketan. In 1933, Tagore published a collection of poems known as *Punashcha*. A poem in that collection is titled 'Patralekha' (writing a letter). The poem is about a newlywed bride trying

---

[110]In the 1970s, Prime Minister Indira Gandhi was gifted an Ebonite pen.

to write a letter to her husband who works somewhere else and begins with the lines, '*[D]ile tumi sona-mora fountain pen*', which translates to, 'You gifted me a gold-wrapped fountain pen'. We do know what happened to Tagore's Eversharp pen, thanks to Bishwanath Ghosh, who writes,

> One day in 1936, when my great-grandfather would regularly accompany Rabindranath Tagore for his evening walks in Shantiniketan, the poet lovingly gifted him an autographed copy of a slim volume of his poems. On another occasion, shortly before the poet died, he gifted my great-grandfather one of his fountain pens—an Eversharp with adjustable nib. Today, the volume of poems occupies a place of pride on my bookshelf in Chennai, but the pen remains mostly locked up, taken out once in a blue moon when I feel poetic and itch to put pen to paper.[111]

We do not quite know whether this was the pen that was stolen from the poet's residence in 1918. It was recovered by the police from the thief, but the police insisted that it was stolen property and could not be handed over to the poet without the permission of the court and that Tagore would have to appear in court as a witness.[112] Eventually, better sense prevailed and he didn't have to.

---

[111]Ghosh, Bishwanath, 'True lies', *The Hindu*, 25 March 2016, https://bit.ly/3wRiJ6a. Accessed on 25 May 2022.

[112]The police released this story from their archives recently. Ghosh, Dwaipayan, 'Read about Rabindranath Tagor's [*sic*] lost pen on Kolkata cops' FB wall', *The Times of India*, 11 December 2017, https://bit.ly/38HFMss. Accessed on 25 May 2022.

## Madras

We have already mentioned Gem and Company from Madras, and chronicled their tale until the end of the 1940s. However, another incident occurred in 1952, when Gem and Company featured in the celebrated Alavandar murder case, which is still widely quoted in Tamil Nadu. After his discharge from the army, Alavandar worked as a salesman for Gem and Company. In the mid-1940s, he branched out on his own, selling plastic and celluloid products, but got some space in front of Gem and Company to sell his products because of his friendship with the founders—Chetty and Cunnan. Though married, Alavandar had a roving eye, and he apparently enticed young women by offering them gifts of expensive fountain pens, which were rare then. One such lady was Devaki, who met Alavandar in mid-1951, when she came to Gem and Company to buy a fountain pen. By 1952, Devaki married a man named Prabhakara Menon and wanted to break off the dalliance with Alavandar. When Alavandar went missing in 1952, Mrs Alavandar lodged a complaint at the police station, and the cops eventually found a head, without a body, floating in the sea. From inside a steel trunk on the Indo-Ceylon Express, a headless body was found. This is where forensic science became important and head and body were identified as belonging to Alavandar. The jury found Devaki and Prabhakara Menon guilty.[113] But let's get back to fountain pens.

---

[113] All the information in this paragraph has been sourced from T.V. Antony Raj's account of the story, which makes it come alive: Raj, T.V. Antony, 'Murder Most Foul', Impressions, 16 October 2013, https://bit.ly/3tj03f1. Accessed on 25 May 2022. A convenient summary of the case can also be found here: Maddy, 'The Alavandar Case', Maddy's Ramblings, 4 June 2016, https://bit.ly/3wKjUpm. Accessed on 9 June 2022. This case is still remembered in Madras and features in books on medical jurisprudence.

## Hyderabad

In Hyderabad, the following pen makers were active: (1) Deccan Pen Stores; (2) Hilal Pen Stores. These have already been discussed earlier.

## Rajahmundry

In Rajahmundry, other than Ratnam, Ratnamson and Brahmam, there was Guider. Guider pens started being manufactured a bit later, in 1946, and were guided by Ratnam. The company website reads:

> This eminent pen company was started under the guidance of experienced persons named Ratnam & Brothers in the year 1946, situated in Rajahmundry bank of the river Godavari in Andhra Prpadesh [*sic*] [...] In the olden days they used to manufacturing [*sic*] manually due to insufficient power supply. The raw material was also imported from Japan. Still the company is having the raw material and pens which [were] made by the professionals above 50 years back. You can choose [from] gold nibbed pens, silver body engraved art pens, celluloid, ebonite, acrylic pens, ball pens & marble stone pens.[114]

## Swadeshi in Ink

Just as the Swadeshi movement brushed off on fountain pens, it affected ink manufacturing as well. After all, a fountain pen cannot function without ink. There was quite a bit of action in

---

[114]"About Us", Guider Pen, https://bit.ly/3PVmJvl. Accessed on 2 June 2022.

the manufacturing of ink too, building on the kind of initiatives we have described in Chapter 2. Camlin, Chelpark and Sulekha are the obvious and big ones, but there were several smaller ones as well. As mentioned in Chapter 2, the 1940s were a period of transition for making and using ink from tablets to liquid ink. There are smaller ink manufacturers one learns about, but we do not always know what happened to them subsequently. Some of these have been listed below.

1.  Mukhi Partabrai registered a trademark for Minister brand in Delhi in 1948, in the name of his minor son, Gordhandas.[115]
2.  Hooghly Ink and Industries was incorporated in 1928. It still exists, but has moved to manufacturing chemicals and chemical products, though it continues to deal in printing ink.
3.  As a diversified group, Kores is a well known name, including for office products. It was incorporated in 1936, to produce carbon-based writing ink and ink tablets.
4.  In 1946, Shiv Shanker Lal Shiv Saran Lal registered Krishna as a trademark for ink, ink tablets and dusts. This is not to be confused with the more famous Krishna ink of recent vintage, associated with the name of Dr Sreekumar. As the family divided, Shiv Shanker Lal Shiv Saran Lal had different successor companies, none of which seem to have anything to do with fountain pens or ink.

---

[115]'Minister', QuickCompany.in, https://bit.ly/3zY0H5B. Accessed on 23 June 2022.

5. National Ink Industries produced a Koel brand of ink tablets.
6. Similarly, S.I.S. Industries from Calcutta produced a brand of ink tablets named Key.
7. In 1947, Suryakant Chandulal Shah registered a trademark for Sailor ink in Bombay.

There are other long-forgotten ink tablets of the same vintage. For example, Swarnamayee's V-2, Paul and Company's Peacock and Jaga Bandhu. Jaga Bandhu Inks began as JBD (Jaga Bandhu Dutta) Inks and was renamed to JBC (Jaga Bandhu Chemical) Inks by the two widows (Lakhsmi and Kshiroda) of the founder—Jaga Bandhu Dutta—after his death. But all these are small manufacturers. The large and more famous ones were Camlin, Chelpark and Sulekha.

Camlin, that is, Dandekar and Company, started production in Bombay in 1931 with ink powders and tablets that were sold under the Horse brand. Since a camel has the reputation for enduring long trips across the desert, Horse was rebranded as Camel. The other rationale for renaming was, '"Camel" was also easy to write and pronounce in all the Indian languages and was acceptable to all the regions of the land.'[116] In 1946, Camel ink became Camlin, and started being produced from a factory in Mahim. In 1946, the enterprise also became a private incorporated company. The enterprise became a public limited company in 1987, and the Japanese company, Kokuyo, acquired a majority stake in it in 2012. Camlin is a recognized brand name across a range of stationery items, not just writing

---

[116]'Heritage', Camlin Kokuyo, https://bit.ly/3sVd1PO. Accessed on 25 May 2022.

instruments or fountain pens. Besides Camlin, over the years, trademarks have been filed for Camlin Yuvak, Camlin Flora, Camlin Supreme, Camlin Regal, Camlin Exam, Camlin Candy, Camlin Nova, Camlin Hyper, Camlin Speedy, Camlin Euro, Camlin Presa, Camlin Kala, Camlin Scholar and Camlin Elegante, not to mention Camlin Kokuyo. Both ink and pens (with Elegante as the non-economy brand) continue to sell.

There were also Chelpark and the ubiquitous Quink brand of fountain pen ink, manufactured by Parker Pen Company. In 1946, Norman Byford used to work for Parker Pen Company in London and looked after Parker's business interests overseas, including Africa. The Chellaram family's business interests can be dated to 1915, when Kishinchand Chellaram established K.K. Chellaram and Sons in Madras. However, K. Chellaram also had extensive business interests in Africa, especially Nigeria. As the anecdote goes, Chellaram bought Parker pens so that they could be sold in Africa. Meanwhile, from 1943, Parker had an Indian venture that made ink, in partnership with the TTK (T.T. Krishnamachari) group. This ink was sold under Parker's famous and ubiquitous brand Quink. When Parker looked for an alternative joint venture partner in India, the Chellaram family had a discussion with Byford and bought the majority shares, with the stipulation that the Chellaram family would not be involved in day-to-day operations. Thus, Chelpark Company Limited was formed in 1953, combining Chellaram and Parker. In the late 1960s and 1970s, the business environment in India was not very kind to international companies, an issue we will return to in subsequent sections. Therefore, Parker exited India in 1969 and Chelpark Company Limited became Chelpark Company Private Limited in 1985, with the headquarters moving from Madras to Bangalore. As for Quink ink, it started being sold as Chelpark, an extremely popular ink at the time. It was so popular that Chelpark Royal Blue ink was used to study plant organs for which staining was necessary.[117] Popular brands of Chelpark fountain pens were Moti, Antic, Brigadier, Fighter and Maverick. Chelpark fountain pens and ink are no longer produced but can be found as collectors' items.

This leaves Sulekha. The Bengali word translates to 'beautiful writing'. Like Ratnam Pens, the trigger for this enterprise was, once again, Gandhiji. His letter, quoted earlier, mentioned a stock of Swadeshi ink.[118] Gandhiji passed on the thought about developing a Swadeshi ink to Satish Chandra Dasgupta, who had retired as the chief chemist of Bengal Chemicals. The thought was passed on to the brothers Sankaracharyya Maitra and Nani Gopal Maitra, who set up the fountain pen manufacturing unit, Sulekha Works Limited, in Rajshahi (now in Bangladesh), in 1934. The first basic formulation of the ink came from Dasgupta. He initially coined the name Krishnadhara, meaning 'black flow'. This was subsequently changed to Sulekha. An urban legend is that the name Sulekha was chosen by Tagore, though there is no actual evidence to substantiate this. After Independence, the company inevitably had to shift to Calcutta. There is a place in the Jadavpur area of Calcutta, famously known

---

[117]There is a remarkable paper on this topic: H.Y. Mohan Ram and Vijay Laxmi Nayyar, 'A Leaf-Clearing Technique with a Wide Range of Applications', *Proceedings of the Indian Academy of Sciences*, Vol. 87 B, (Plant Sciences-2), No. 5, 1978.
[118]Gandhi, M.K., *Mahatma Gandhi's Collected Works*, Vol. 58, Gandhi Sevagram Ashram, https://bit.ly/3xxPk2J. Accessed on 9 June 2022.

as Sulekha More, or 'Sulekha Crossroads', named after the company. Sulekha became ubiquitous in the eastern parts of India, though there was a manufacturing unit in Ghaziabad too. In terms of chronology, we are jumping the gun a bit. However, by the end of the 1970s, Sulekha not only had a strong presence within the country, it exported its expertise to other South Asian and African countries as well.

In the late 1980s, Sulekha had to shut shop due, in part, to trade unionism. Sulekha restarted in 2005, initially in unrelated sectors, such as solar power. One should not think that Sulekha only manufactured ink. It made pens too, reasonably cheap ones. Given the heading of this section, it is important to emphasize a point that is often missed. Sulekha advertisements were everywhere. However, though Sulekha's roots were Swadeshi, it never harped on Swadeshi in its advertisements.

It would also be interesting to note that Sulekha Ink never exploited the nationalist sentiment although it too started manufacturing ink in 1934 as a part of the Nationalist project. In its advertisements, Sulekha mentioned the brightness of the colour of the ink and later its waterproof quality [...] To outdo the competitors, the appeal to give up the 'infatuation' for foreign ink was pointless for Sulekha.[119]

This was in marked contrast with Supra Ink. Historically, Supra Ink advertisements had harped on the nationalist angle. Supra Pens was another company that has completely moved away from fountain pens and fountain pen ink to toilets and

---

[119]Ghosh, Chilka, *Printed Advertisement 1947-1970: Bengali Middleclass; An Interaction*, Cambridge Scholars Publishing, 2014.

chemicals, where the Supra brand name is still used. However, in 1956, Super Toilet and Chemical Company registered this trademark for ink as well.

With a name like Sulekha, it was inevitable that there would be a legal question about whether Sulekha could be registered as a trademark since a name that has a general meaning is not granted intellectual property right protection. There was indeed such a case, but later, after Independence. In January 1961, Justice A.P. Shah ruled in favour of Sulekha Works. It is worth quoting from the judgement, although the quote will be somewhat long. The quote establishes who, or what, the owners of Sulekha named their ink and pen after.

> A short but rather an interesting question has been raised on this petition and the question is as to whether the word 'Sulekha' which was registered as a trade mark by the Registrar of Trade Marks as far back as on 4th May 1953, in connection with fountain pens, nibs, etc., which were being manufactured by the petitioners means 'good writing' so that it amounts to a description of the fountain pens and other materials manufactured by the petitioners, in which event, that word would not be registrable as a trade mark. It appears that the petitioners started the business of manufacturing fountain pens and other materials some time in 1951. They dealt in these fountain pens and other materials as 'Sulekha' fountain pens and materials. On 8th January, 1952 the petitioners applied to the Registrar of Trade Marks for registration of the word 'Sulekha' as a trade mark in connection with the fountain pens and other materials that they were manufacturing and dealing in. After the necessary enquiry under the Trade Marks Act

by an order dated 4th May, 1953, the application made by the petitioners was granted and the word 'Sulekha' was registered as a trade mark in connection with the petitioners' fountain pens and other connected materials. It may be noted that in the application that was made for the registration of the trade mark, the petitioners had stated that 'Sulekha' was the name of a female and at the hearing of the application evidence was led to show [*sic*] that that word had attained a distinctive character in relation to their fountain pens and other materials. No contention then appears to have been raised either by the Registrar of Trade Marks, or by any member of the public that the word 'Sulekha' was in any way or in any sense descriptive of the pens that were being manufactured by the petitioners so as to indicate their nature or quality. The Registrar, apparently, was satisfied that the word was in vogue as the name of a female person and also that it had obtained a distinctive character by reason of the petitioners having dealt in the pens and other materials manufactured by them under that name. It was only after the Registrar was thus satisfied that he had passed the order for registration of the word 'Sulekha' as a trademark in connection with the petitioners' fountain pens and other connected materials. On 6th February, 1956, however, it appears, the Registrar of Trade Marks, who apparently was not the same gentleman who had ordered the registration of the trade mark in 1953 gave a notice to the petitioners calling upon them to show cause as to why the register of trade marks should not be rectified by expunging therefrom the entry relating to the trade mark No. 152234 in relation to the word

'Sulekha' in exercise of his powers under section 46 (4) of the Trade Marks Act, for the reason that in his opinion the word 'Sulekha' meant 'good writing' and that it was not adopted to distinguish goods in respect of which it was registered, namely, fountain pens, pencils, pen-holders, and parts thereof.[120]

Sulekha was named after a lady, though the expression also means 'good writing'. The court ruled that the Registrar of Trade Marks should not have opened the issue again, after having initially granted the trademark.

Initially, Sulekha also produced ink dust and ink tablets. Bottled and liquid ink was sold under three brand names— Sulekha Executive Ink, Sulekha Special and Sulekha General, with varying sizes of bottles. Though Sulekha also produced fountain pens, it was primarily known for its ink. With the benefit of hindsight, Sulekha erred in pursuing trademarks primarily for ink tablets, ink dust and writing ink, and not for fountain pens. Prior to 1940, there was no codified trademark legislation in India. Common law principles were invoked. The Trade Marks Act was passed in 1940, later subsumed in the Trade and Merchandise Marks Act of 1958. As the quote above illustrates, in 1952/1953, Sulekha was registered as a trademark for both ink and writing instruments. Registration is, of course, not mandatory. More importantly, registration is for a limited period of time and has to be renewed. Registrations seem to have been pursued in the 1960s and 1970s, as device trademarks for ink and not for writing instruments. Meanwhile, after Sulekha closed down in the 1980s, in 1988, through the

---

[120]'J.L. Mehta Versus Registrar of Trade Marks', Lawyerservices, https://bit.ly/3NyBmCH. Accessed on 25 May 2022.

Madras office, Pukhraj Jain and Raju Thomas independently filed applications to register the trademark Sulekha. Both applications covered pens (ballpoint pens as well as fountain pens) but excluded ink.[121] These Sulekha pens, produced by Jain or Thomas, were different from the original Sulekha pens. Subsequently, the original Sulekha was revived under the name of 'New Sulekha Industries' and the Sulekha trademark was registered for both fountain pens and ink. This was possible because trademarks, such as those granted to Jain or Thomas, are registered for limited periods of time. Indeed, Jain's successors failed to re-register the Sulekha trademark.

However, as we end this chapter, let us emphasize that ink production was not only about manufacturers like Camlin, Chelpark and Sulekha. When World War II dislocated supplies from abroad, there were many units that started to produce fountain pen ink and catered to the demand, both civil and military. Be that as it may, at the time of Independence, the 'Indian' and the 'foreign' coexisted, and there was no reason for India to not have established its presence in manufacturing fountain pens, its nibs and ink. Our base was superior to many other countries that became centres of fountain pen manufacture later. However, policy proved to be a hindrance and prevented that take-off. This is the story of unmake in India.

---

[121]'MCA Services: Company/LLP Master Data', Ministry of Corporate Affairs, https://bit.ly/3xuD55F. Accessed on 15 June 2022.

# 5

## THE AUTARKY FETTER: THE 1950s AND 1960s

Before the whiff of reforms and liberalization, there used to be a wisecrack about Indian fountain pens being more fountains than pens. The fountain pen promise failed to materialize in India due to policy-induced distortions. Before we come to the policy-induced distortions, we need to convey the flavour of the times in so far as economic policymaking was concerned. In this chapter, we will focus on how, as part of the autarky fetter, imports were controlled, regulated and eventually prohibited, to prevent competition from abroad.

### Congress and Planning

The 1931 Karachi resolution of the Indian National Congress (INC) was important because it articulated notions of fundamental rights and also had a view on what the State should do, including its economic and social programmes. For example, 'The State shall protect indigenous cloth; and for this purpose, pursue the policy of exclusion of foreign cloth and foreign yarn from the country and adopt such other measures as may be found necessary. The State shall also protect other indigenous industries, when necessary, against foreign competition' and, 'The State shall own or control key industries and services, mineral resources, railways, waterways, shipping, and other means of public transport.'[122] A view about the role of the State was developing, and this inevitably led to the need for planning. A Working Committee of the INC in Wardha in 1937 recommended, '[...]to the Congress Ministries the appointment of a Committee of Experts to consider urgent and vital problems the solution of which is necessary to any scheme of national reconstruction and social planning.' All this led to the formation of the National Planning Committee in 1938, chaired by Jawaharlal Nehru.[123] Since a separate agrarian programme was to exist, 'plan' was tantamount to an industrial plan.

In 1938, there was a conference of industry ministers in Delhi, under the chairmanship of Subhash Chandra Bose, the then president of the INC. This meeting passed the following resolution. 'As a step towards such industrialisation, a comprehensive scheme of national planning should be formulated. This scheme should provide for the development of heavy key industries, medium scale industries and cottage industries, keeping in view our national requirements, the resources of the country, as also the peculiar circumstances

---

[122]'Karachi Resolution 1931', Abhijeet Singh, https://bit.ly/3NZFLzh. Accessed on 15 June 2022.

[123]This National Planning Committee never published any reports. However, several details about its meetings are available in the following source: Shah, K.T., *National Planning Committee: Being an Abstract of Proceedings and Other Particulars Relating to the National Planning Committee*, Bombay, 1948, https://bit.ly/3aaHbb6. Accessed on 25 May 2022. All the quotations in this paragraph have been taken from this source.

prevailing in the country.'[124] Obviously, one would have needed to identify what these key heavy industries were, and an answer was given:

> This Conference [...] is of the opinion that pending the submission and consideration of a comprehensive industrial plan for the whole of India, steps should be taken to start the following large scale industries of national importance on an all-India basis and the efforts of all provinces and Indian States, should as far as possible, be coordinated to that end: (a) Manufacture of machinery and plant and tools of all kinds; (b) Manufacture of automobiles, motor boats, etc., and their accessories and other industries connected with transport and communication; (c) Manufacture of electrical plant and accessories; (d) Manufacture of heavy chemicals and fertilizers; (e) Metal production; (f) Industries connected with power generation and power supply.[125]

It is unreasonable to expect expressions like 'market failure' to be used then. But, if one applies today's jargon to that period, these industries were characterized by market failure. Whatever be the reason, private capital would not step in. The National Planning Committee also recommended the establishment of an All-India National Planning Commission.[126]

---

[124]Shah, K.T., *National Planning Committee: Being an Abstract of Proceedings and Other Particulars Relating to the National Planning Committee*, Bombay, 1948, https://bit.ly/3aaHbb6. Accessed on 25 May 2022.
[125]Ibid.
[126]Ibid.

With this interest in planning, it should not be surprising that, during this period, several plans were developed, independent of the National Planning Committee, such as: M. Visvesvaraya's Plan;[127] the Bombay Plan;[128] the People's Plan;[129] the Gandhian Plan[130] and the Sarvodaya Plan.[131] In many portrayals of the history of economic development and planning in post-Independence India, it is often suggested that there was a sudden discontinuity with the five year plans, in particular the Second Five Year Plan (1956–61). This is not quite true. Though these diverse plans differed in individual aspects, across the plans, there was consensus on (a) public investments in key industries; (b) state intervention in distribution to prevent a widening of income disparities and (c) peripheral roles of external trade and foreign investments. These tenets represented the wisdom of the day.

---

[127]Visvesvaraya, M., *Planned Economy for India,* Bangalore Press, Bangalore, 1934.

[128]Thakurdas, Purushotamdas and Jehangir Ratanji Dadabhoy Tata, *Memorandum Outlining a Plan of Economic Development for India,* Penguin, 1944 and 1945. It was published in two parts.

[129]Banerjee, B.N., et al., *People's Plan for Economic Development of India,* The Post-war Reconstruction Committee of Indian Federation of Labour, 1944, https://bit.ly/3mATS1Q. Accessed on 10 June 2022. This initiative was driven by M.N. Roy.

[130]Agarwal, S.N., *The Gandhian Plan of Economic Development for India,* Padma Publications, 1944.

[131]*Principles of Sarvodaya Plan,* Sarvodaya Planning Committee, 1950. Most plans, other than Sarvodaya, naturally presumed a pre-Partition geography for India.

## The Industrial Policy Resolution: Two Versions

In 1948, the Industrial Policy Resolution was adopted by the government. For industry, this clearly articulated the principles of complete State monopoly over some sectors, State monopoly for new enterprises in other sectors, possible nationalization of existing private sector enterprises and majority Indian equity in instances involving foreign capital. By 1948, the building blocks of a mixed economy, public sector monopolies, State controls and import-substitution were already in place. Statutory formalization of these principles came through the Industries (Development and Regulation) Act (IDRA) of 1951. The Bill was ready in 1949 and mentioned the central government's powers to license new undertakings and register and regulate existing ones. A few quotes may help illustrate what this piece of legislation achieved. Section 2 of the Act stated, 'It is here by declared that it is expedient in the public interest that the Union should take under its control the industries specified in the First Schedule.'[132] Eventually, almost everything one can think of came to be included in the First Schedule. Section 11 stated:

> No person or authority other than the Central Government, shall, after the commencement of this Act, establish any new industrial undertaking, except under and in accordance with a license issued in that behalf by the Central Government [...] A license or permission [...] may contain such conditions including, in particular,

---

[132]'The Industries (Development and Regulation) Act, 1951', Legislative Department | Ministry of Law and Justice | Government of India, https://bit.ly/39SlZX7. Accessed on 25 May 2022.

conditions as to the location of the undertaking and the minimum standard in respect of size to be provided therein as the Central Government may deem fit to impose in accordance with the rules.[133]

Bits and pieces would continue to be added to the 1951 statute. For instance, a 1953 amendment gave the central government powers to assume control of an existing industrial undertaking. That amendment also gave the central government powers to control supply, distribution and prices. In books on economic policymaking, rarely is there a reference to statutes, though they provide the backing for the policy. The recent book by Gautam Chikermane titled *70 Policies that Shaped India* is one of these rare exceptions.[134]

In the list of statutes that form the bedrock of economic policy, the most important is the Constitution, enacted in 1950. Of course, today's Constitution is not identical to the Constitution that was adopted in 1949 and enacted in 1950.

---

[133]Ibid.

[134]Chikermane, Gautam, *70 Policies that Shaped India*, Observer Research Foundation, 2018, https://bit.ly/3PFcpaK. Accessed on 25 May 2022. 'India's infamous License Raj began here [...] The First Schedule included 38 industries, from defense and machine tools to telecommunications and electrical equipment; and 171 articles, from precious metals and coal to fans and sewing machines.' All those 171 articles mentioned by Chikermane were not part of the First Schedule in 1951. They were incrementally added. The original First Schedule had 37 heads, it increased to 42 in 1953. Over time, the heads were also reclassified, so one cannot simply look at the number of headings and deduce an increase in the importance of IDRA. For instance, in 1951, hurricane lanterns were a separate heading. Later, they became an item under the head of commercial, office and household equipment.

This was the context in which the Planning Commission was set up through a Cabinet Resolution dated 15 March 1950. The First Five Year Plan was developed for the period between 1951 and 1956.

Towards the end of 1955, Milton Friedman visited India and was an adviser to the then Finance Minister C.D. Deshmukh. In a memorandum to the Government of India, he wrote,

> There is a tendency not only in India but in most of the literature on economic development to regard the ratio of investment national income as almost the only key to the rate of development to take it for granted that there is a rigid and mechanical ratio between the amount of investment and additions to output [...] There are two reasons why the amount of investment and the increase in output can be, and empirically are, only loosely connected. First, the form and distribution of investment are at least as important as its sheer magnitude. Second, what is called capital investment is only part of the total expenditure on increasing the productivity of an economy [...] The form of investment is no less important than its kind. The chief problem in the Indian program that impresses on the tendency to concentrate investment in heavy industry at one extreme and handicrafts at the other, at the expense of small and moderate size industry. This policy threatens an inefficient use of capital at the one extreme by combining it with too little labour and an inefficient use of labour at the other extreme by combining it with too little capital [...] The areas for which only Government can take responsibility are here so large, so vital, and require such large investments that they alone would be a heavy

burden on the limited administrative personnel of high calibre. It seems the better part of wisdom therefore to avoid any activities that can be left to others. [135]

In 1955, preparations for the Second Five Year Plan (1956–61), which had begun in 1954, were in full swing, and the plan document was finalized by March 1956. At that time, V.T. Krishnamachari was the deputy chairman of the Planning Commission. P.C. Mahalanobis became a member in January 1955 and remained a member till September 1967. In most discussions of the Second Five Year Plan, the Plan was equated with the Feldman–Mahalanobis model. The Soviet economist, Grigory Feldman, developed this model in 1928, though it was translated into English much later. The first Mahalanobis version was a two-sector model, published in 1953.[136] Shorn of the algebra, in a closed economy, there are two sectors—consumer goods and capital goods. Investments can be in either. High investment shares in consumer goods lead to high output initially but eventually yield low output. Therefore, in the long run, it is better to channel investments into capital goods, which can be equated with heavy industry.

This model stimulated a great deal of interest among economists and, over a period of time, criticisms and alternative models surfaced with regular periodicity. It is possible to be contrarian and argue that the model was not quite the

---

[135]Shah, Parth J. (ed.), *Friedman on India*, Centre for Civil Society, 2000, https://bit.ly/3tqYM5g. Accessed on 10 June 2022.

[136]Mahalanobis, P.C., 'Some Observations on the Process of Growth of National Income', *Sankhya*, Vol. 12, No. 4, 1953. A subsequent four-sector model (1955) was also developed that sub-divided the consumer goods sector into three sub-categories.

defining attribute of the Second Five Year Plan. Economists love mathematics, algebra and rigour, and here was a model one could lay one's hands on, even if one disagreed with its assumptions. However, apart from the obvious emphasis on heavy industry, the defining attribute of the Second Five Year Plan lay elsewhere. The Avadi session of the INC was held in 1955, which led to a resolution declaring that a socialistic pattern of society was the explicit goal. The Industrial Policy Resolution of 1948 was replaced by a new Industrial Policy Resolution of 1956, which stated:

> This policy must be governed by the principles laid down in the Constitution, the objective of socialism, and the experience gained during these years [...] The adoption of the socialist pattern of society as the national objective, as well as the need for planned and rapid development, require that all industries of basic and strategic importance, or in the nature of public utility services, should be in the public sector. Other industries which are essential and require investment on a scale which only the State, in present circumstances, could provide, have also to be in the public sector.[137]

The Planning Commission and the Second Five Year Plan document were part of this jigsaw. The First Five Year plan document may have referred to the Directive Principles of State Policy but it had not used the expression 'socialist pattern of society'. The Second Five Year Plan document began with this expression. That was the critical difference, not the model.

---

[137]'2nd Five Year Plan', NITI Aayog, https://bit.ly/3NCdnm2. Accessed on 25 May 2022.

## Import Duties and Plans: Seeds for the Future

The seeds had been sown for public and private monopolies leading to protected domestic markets and inefficiencies; for import substitution; for export subsidies to ensure that inefficient domestic enterprise survived in competitive global markets; for the neglect of agriculture consumer goods and small-scale industries. And perhaps, most devastating of all, the seeds had been sown for a maze of controls and regulations. This led to the State clamping down on imports, through quantitative restrictions (QRs) and tariffs and enforcing licensing, which prevented fresh entry of goods.

In 1958, a journalist named Alexander Campbell published a book on India titled *The Heart of India*. This book has never been published or printed in India and its imports into India have been banned.[138] It is an extremely patronizing book, though that should hardly be a reason for a ban. There is a section in it about a meeting with Vaidya Sharma of the Ministry of Planning.

> He [Vaidya Sharma] put away the housing-development papers, and talked again about the Five Year Plan. 'We have now entered the period of the second Plan. The first Plan built up our food resources; the second Plan will lay the foundations for rapid creation of heavy industry. Delhi, as the capital of India, will play a big part, and we are getting ready to shoulder the burden. We are going to build a big central stationery depot, with a special

---

[138]'A. Prohibited items under Exim Policy (S.No. 4901)', Customs Tariff Database Online, Ministry of Finance, Government of India, https://bit.ly/39do7sV. Accessed on 10 June 2022.

railway-siding of its own. There will be no fewer than 12 halls, each covering 2,000 square feet. They will be storage halls, and,' said Sharma triumphantly, 'we calculate that the depot will be capable of an annual turnover of 1,400 tons of official forms, forms required for carrying out the commitments of the second Five Year Plan!'[139]

This might very well be concocted and exaggerated, but there is a grain of truth somewhere.

Across models and views of that era, (a) external trade was unimportant; (b) consumer goods were unimportant. As consumer goods, fountain pens were also relatively unimportant. Oddly enough, there was a committee with a slightly different view: the Export Promotion Committee in 1949. It is rarely mentioned, but its take makes for refreshing reading.

It is somewhat paradoxical that, while the Government has been aiming at export drive, elaborate machinery to exercise control over the majority of exports exists. The present export control notification has been inherited from the days of the war when there was need to restrict the volume of exports for a variety of reasons, many of which no longer hold good [...] When we have to depend on imports to supply us with food and fertilizers, raw materials and machinery, the necessary foreign exchange for which is not being earned by our present level of exports, clearly the case for reducing as far as possible all restrictions on our export trade is overwhelming [...] We are aware that clocks and watches are mostly of hard currency (Swiss) origin. Watches, however, have to

---

[139]Campbell, Alexander, *The Heart of India,* Alfred A. Knopf, 1958.

be imported at the cost of hard currency, not primarily because we must have them, but because the Swiss insist that if we take other things from them which we really need, we must also take some watches, the export of which forms part of their traditional pattern of trade. In our view, it is desirable that these watches should be exported so that the hard currency spent on them may not mean a total loss of foreign exchange but only of hard currency, soft currency being obtained in substitution. [140]

In a similar vein, the committee spoke about 'Indian assembled American cars' being re-exported to third countries. The committee did not specifically mention fountain pens. They were not important enough. However, if India could export watches and cars, why not fountain pens and fountain pen inks? All of these were consumer goods.

The class composition of those who set up units to manufacture fountain pens was probably somewhat different from the class composition of those who set up units to manufacture fountain pen ink. At least, that's what the Tariff Board report suggests.[141] Therefore, there seems to have been more political interest in fountain pen ink than in fountain pens. Accordingly, on 30 August 1948, a question was asked in the Constituent Assembly on the manufacture and import of printing and fountain pen ink. The Minister of Commerce (K.C. Neogy) was asked about (a) the quantity and value of

---

[140]'Report of the Export Promotion Committee', Indian Culture, 1949, https://bit.ly/3mC50vE. Accessed on 10 June 2022.
The Chairman of this committee was A.D. Gorwala.
[141]'Report on the Fountain Pen Ink Industry August 1949', Indian Culture, 1949, https://bit.ly/3xAvAeN. Accessed on 10 June 2022.

fountain pen ink imported into India in 1946 and 1947; (b) the value of such ink being manufactured in India; (c) whether there were sufficient technicians in India who could manufacture fountain pen ink that could successfully compete with imported ink; and (d) the quantity and value of printing ink—imported and domestically made. The Minister answered that fountain pen ink was manufactured in India and there were technicians in India who could make good quality ink. However, there were no figures on fountain pen ink—imported or domestic. He gave some figures on imports of printers' and lithographers' ink.[142]

However, in 1950, the Tariff Board produced a report on the fountain pen ink industry, which has an excellent description of the state of the fountain pen ink industry and illustrates the kind of calculation that went into computing import duties to ensure a level playing field:

The first factory established in India to produce fountain pen ink on a commercial scale was the Krishnaveni Inks set up in Madras in 1920 [...] Between 1920 and 1930, a few more units were established in the State of Madras and elsewhere. During the period from 1930 to 1940, ten more units were established in different parts of the country. Thus, before World War II, there were more than a dozen indigenous factories producing fountain pen ink. It was, however, the advent of World War II that gave a stimulus to this industry to develop rapidly. This was mainly due to the disorganization of world trade and lack of shipping

---

[142]'The Constituent Assembly of India (Legislative) Debates (Part I-Questions and Answers) | Official Report Volume VI. 1948 (9th August to 31st August. 1948)', Parliament of India, Lok Sabha Digital Library, 1948, https://bit.ly/3mBcnmY. Accessed on 10 June 2022.

facilities, resulting in the reduction of imports of fountain pen ink. The indigenous industry which had so far suffered from keen competition from the imported inks now began to meet not only the requirements of the civilian population but also those of the two million personnel of the defence services stationed in the country. During this period, the indigenous producers also exported the article to the neighbouring Eastern countries. It will thus be seen that the main expansion of this industry took place during war-time and the immediate post-war period [...] However, during the early post-war period, the production of indigenous fountain pen ink was considerably curtailed due to the keen competition offered by large quantities of the imported material which was being sold at comparatively low rates. We have, however, been informed by the industry that as a result of the total banning of imports of fountain pen ink since July, 1949, the position of the industry has improved during the last few months [...] The number of known units at present is about seventy-seven, and they are distributed all over the country, but South India and the States of Bengal and Bombay claim the largest numbers. The industry is mainly composed of small units. The amount of capital employed in the different units ranges from Rs. 250 to Rs. 2 lakhs; in the majority of cases, however, the amount invested is below Rs. 20,000. The number of workers employed in the different units varies from 2 to 5 and in a few cases from 10 to 50. It may also be noted that the industry has been established mainly by educated middle class people with comparatively small financial resources. [...] The countries from which fountain pen inks are mainly

*Dr Radhika Nath Saha, the creator of the first Indian fountain pen*

*F.N. Gooptu fountain pen and box*

*J.B. Dutt box of ink tablets, carrying the only known picture of Jaga Bandhu Dutt*

*Ink tablet boxes for Krishna, Sulekha and JCD*

*Luxmi fountain and stylo pens*

F.N. Gooptu, an early major manufacturer of fountain pens and nibs

Kajal Kali advertisement from the 1930s

দুইশত বছরের তমসার শেষে জেগে উঠছে নবীন প্রভাত। আর তারি আভায় প্রতিভাত হচ্ছে নবজীবনের সুবিপুল সম্ভাবনা—সুখ, সমৃদ্ধি, আশা ও আনন্দের পরিপূর্ণ মূর্তরূপ।

এই নবযুগের প্রথম শারদীয় উৎসবে আজ আবার নতুন করে আমাদের শুভানুধ্যায়ী ও সহৃদয় পৃষ্ঠপোষকদের জানাচ্ছি অকুণ্ঠ অভিনন্দন ও অফুরন্ত শুভেচ্ছা।

কপিং, ড্রইং ও যাবতীয় লেড পেন্সিল, কলম, নিব এবং ফাউন্টেন পেন

প্রস্তুতকারক জি. সি. ল ও কোং কর্তৃক প্রচারিত

ভারতবর্ষ, ব্রহ্মদেশ, সিংহল, সুদূরপ্রাচ্য, মধ্যপ্রাচ্য ও অস্ট্রেলিয়ার একমাত্র পরিবেশক:—
জি. অ্যাথারটন এণ্ড কোং লিঃ
৭নং মিশন রো, কলিকাতা।

G.C. Law advertisement, dated 15 August 1947

*Das Boral's Lekhani advertisement from 1947*

*Artex pens*

*Ratnamson fountain pens*

*Diploma fountain pens*

*Ruby fountain pens*

*Guider fountain pens*

*Wilson fountain pens*

*Kingson fountain pens*

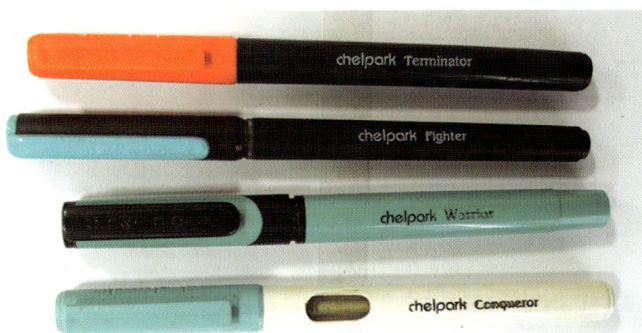

*Chelpark fountain pens*

*President fountain pens*

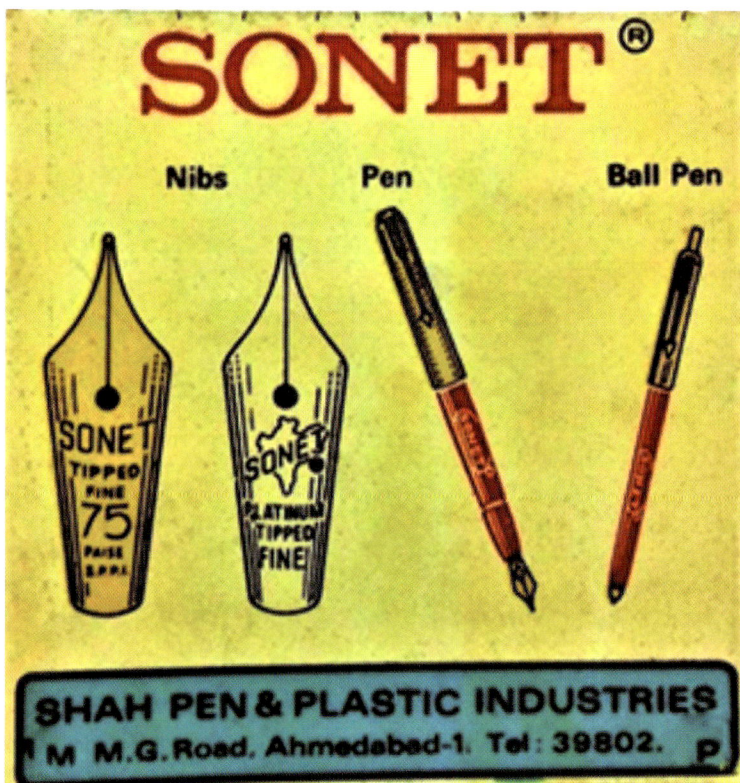

*Advertisement for Sonet pens and nibs*

*Pilot fountain pens that were made in India*

*Dayal Bagh fountain pen, manufactured by Model Industries*

*Airmail-Wality fountain pens*

*Bril ink*

*Ambitious fountain pens*

*Click fountain pens*

*Gama fountain pens*

*Ranga fountain pens*

*Kanwrite fountain pens*

*Assorted low-end current Indian pens*

*Camlin fountain pens*

An advertisement for Dr R.N. Saha pens

Kim and Company fountain pen from Kerala

Bharati fountain pen

*Camlin fountain pen*

*Micro fountain pen*

*Flair fountain pen*

*National fountain pen*

*Jupiter fountain pen*

*Capital fountain pen*

*Mebsons fountain pen*

*Bachelor fountain pen*

*Wesco fountain pens*

*BigBen fountain pens*

*Tiger fountain pens*

imported into India are U.K. and U.S.A. The brands of imported ink which are popular in the country are 'Swan', 'Waterman', 'Quink', 'Skrip' and 'Stephens' [...] It will be seen that fountain pen ink was on O.G.L. During the period January-June, 1949. The manufacturers stated before us that this liberal licensing policy resulted in large imports of the article being brought into the country and heavy stocks built up, which will last for a considerable time [...] Since, however, the entire needs of the Indian Union can be met by the indigenous manufacturers, we recommend that so long as the policy of licensing has to be continued for balance of payment considerations, the desirability of maintaining and expanding the indigenous production of fountain pen ink should be kept in view and the quantum of imports regulated accordingly.[143]

The report recommended an import duty of 37.5 per cent on imports of fountain pen ink. This would, according to the report, 'cover the difference between the estimated fair selling price of the indigenous product and the landed cost without duty of the imported article [...] Moreover, as long as the present import control continues, it will also serve as a most effective measure of protection to the industry and give it an

---

[143]'Report on the Fountain Pen Ink Industry August 1949', Indian Culture, 1949, https://bit.ly/3xAvAeN. Accessed on 10 June 2022. The innocuous sounding expression about 'educated middle class people' in the quote may have had significant implications in terms of being able to lobby and create protectionist pressures, much more than by fountain pen makers. Skrip is made by Sheaffer and Stephens means Henry C. Stephens. In the quote, OGL stands for open general licence.

opportunity to improve its power of competition.'[144] There cannot have been a better articulation of the infant industry and import substitution argument.

The report mentioned a list of 82 producers.[145] Based on this estimate, these producers were obviously the larger ones. There was a long list of importers too. The list does not mention Daytone Stationery Products, started in 1956, probably because at that time, Daytone's import substitution was in drawing ink, not fountain pen ink.

Tariff protection was generally not perceived to be adequate, as an editorial from the influential *Economic and Political Weekly*, written in 1953, shows.[146] The gist of the argument was that tariff protection encouraged foreign manufacturers to jump tariffs and set up manufacturing enterprises in India. For example, there was the Japanese Pilot and the American Parker. Small Indian manufacturers had no chance of competing against them. Therefore, they sought a ban on establishment of foreign enterprises. It is understandable that inefficient production should lobby for protection. But independent commentary also supported the idea. Such were the times. As the article states:

> It is difficult to understand how these two foreign units managed to, 'jump over' the tariff wall and establish themselves comfortably, thus negating the very idea of protection to the domestic industry [...] Subsequent

[144]'Report on the Fountain Pen Ink Industry August 1949', Indian Culture, 1949, https://bit.ly/3xAvAeN. Accessed on 10 June 2022.
[145]See Appendix I for the complete list.
[146]'Made in India, Plight of Fountain Pen Ink Industry', *Economic and Political Weekly*, Vol. 5, No. 29, 18 July 1953, https://bit.ly/3MSaoWd. Accessed on 25 May 2022.

legislation on the subject is incorporated in the Development of Industries (Control and Regulation) Act which provides that all new units for Scheduled industries will require a license. What about industries outside the Schedule? Apparently in such cases restrictions are last, even that about control of management being predominantly in Indian hands. How else to explain that the Parker Fountain Pen Company (India) Ltd of course, which has set up manufacture of inks can have 60 per cent of American capital?[147]

Tariffs become relevant only if an item can be freely imported. Until QRs on imports were eventually eliminated and replaced by tariffs, most imported items required an import licence. Few items were on an open general licence (OGL). The expression OGL, used in Indian export and import policy, is a bit of an oxymoron. Contrary to a normal English language interpretation of the term, OGL actually meant that a licence was not required. Anyone could freely import a product, subject to the payment of appropriate import duties. Stated simply, items were divided into OGL—restricted (where a specific import licence was required) and prohibited. OGL was a bit like a positive list. If an item was not on the list, it specifically required a license for importing. In those early years, much of legislation and policy was inherited from a period of wartime shortages and the 1939 Defence of India Act. This was also true of the Imports and Exports (Control) Act of 1947, which gave those licensing powers to the government, operating through Ministry of Commerce and Department of Foreign Trade. This

---

[147]Ibid.

was 'An Act to prohibit or control imports and exports' because 'it is expedient to prohibit, restrict or otherwise control imports and exports'.[148] Interestingly, when the legislation was originally enacted in 1947, the qualification of 'for a limited period' was attached to it. This bit was excised in 1971. Thus, as was true of many other pieces of legislation, statutes meant to be temporary were entered into the statute books permanently.

## Importing Pens: Agreement with China

Fountain pens are consumer goods. Therefore, free imports of fountain pens, without licensing, had to wait till April 2001, when India phased out all QRs on imports. India has been a founding member of the General Agreement on Tariffs and Trade (GATT) since its formation in 1948. GATT principles prohibit the use of QRs. Specifically, though, there are some exemptions, Article XI of GATT prohibits QRs on both exports and imports. However, Article XVIII Section B allows leeway to countries that face balance of payments (BoP) problems. Such countries can deviate from that principle of eliminating QRs. This provision did not exist in the original GATT agreement, signed in 1948. It was brought into Article XVIII during the GATT review session in 1954–55, reflecting special and differential treatment to developing countries. Once this had been done, in 1954, India invoked Article XVIII Section B and sought the flexibility to impose QRs on imports.[149] This waiver

---

[148]'Imports and Exports (Control) Act 1947', IndianLegislation, https://bit.ly/3LEJH6A. Accessed on 25 May 2022.
[149]'India and GATT', *Economic and Political Weekly*, Vol. 7, No. 40, 20 March 1954, https://bit.ly/3yVSlLe. Accessed on 25 May 2022.

from commitments was sought for eight items: (a) canned fish; (b) wines; (c) tooth paste, tooth powder, talcum powder, shaving soap and shaving cream; (d) lithopone; (e) coal-tar dyes; (f) glass beads and false pearls and (g) safety razors and parts. Besides these seven items, the eighth was fountain pens and parts. If nothing else, this illustrates how important fountain pens were perceived to be in 1954. Like all those other items in that initial list of 1954 under Article XVIII Section B, these items were consumer goods. However, every conceivable consumer good did not feature in that 1954 list. There was no mention of cars or watches, for example.

This being the case, the trade agreement signed between Indian and the People's Republic of China (PRC) in October 1954 was somewhat odd—an agreement that existed in the same form till 1959.[150] This agreement included a list of goods China could export to India, a list of goods India could export to China and a separate list of goods India could export to 'the Tibet Region of China'. Bilateral agreements are the outcome of negotiations. To get something you want, you yield on others. There is quid pro quo and reciprocity. Gains and losses need not always be defined in narrow economic terms, the quid and the quo can be strategic. However, a quid without the quo does not sound rational. Outside the then socialist bloc, India was the first country to establish diplomatic relations with the PRC. This happened on 1 January 1950, and Pakistan followed a few days later by establishing diplomatic relations with the PRC. India followed through, in October 1954, with

---

[150]'Trade Agreement Between the Republic of India and the People's Republic of China', Ministry of External Affairs, 14 October 1954, https://bit.ly/3amaVlz. Accessed on 25 May 2022.

a trade agreement with the PRC, apparently based on 'equality and mutual benefit'. At least, that is what the preamble to the agreement said. As part of this trade agreement, many historical rights India possessed (trade missions/trading posts) in Tibet were signed away. Therefore, for the benefit to be mutual and not unilateral, India must have gained something. This was a narrow trade agreement. Unlike contemporary times, there was no talk of cross-border labour or capital movements. The gains could have been trade or non-trade.

In any such trade agreement, while negotiating, negotiators try to identify products where their country has a comparative advantage, though comparative advantage is necessarily dynamic and changes over time. One tries to get market access for items where the home country is competitive and tries to bargain and prevent granting market access for items where the home country is relatively uncompetitive. This is the principle behind trade negotiations. Broadly, China was allowed to export: (a) cereals; (b) machinery; (c) minerals; (d) silk and silk piece-goods; (e) animal products; (f) paper and stationery; (g) chemicals; (h) oils; and (i) miscellaneous items. India was allowed to export: (a) grams, rice, pulses; (b) kyanite; (c) unmanufactured tobacco; (d) raw materials and unmanufactured ores; (e) wood and timber; (f) hides and skins; (g) chemicals; (h) vehicles; and (i) miscellaneous items. At that time, both countries were planning to industrialize—China with a first five year plan in 1953 and India with a first five year plan in 1951. That being the case, one would expect aspirations for industrialization, and moving away from agriculture, to be reflected in the items either side was trying to push. If one looks at those broad headings, this is not the impression one gets. For example, India would export wood and timber, but China would export paper and stationery. China would export machinery, but India would export raw materials and unmanufactured ores. That is, barring chemicals and vehicles, India would remain a primary produce exporter to China—a continuing trend this trade agreement contributed to. However, China's exports would be broad-based and include manufacturing. The items mentioned above were broad headings. Those were not the days when trade negotiators followed harmonized customs nomenclatures, with digits pinning down items. Such physical descriptions sufficed. As part of these broad headings, the items included under paper and stationery were: (a) newsprint; (b) mechanical pulp-free printing paper; (c) packing paper; (d) stencil paper; (e) blotting paper; (f) fountain pens; (g) pencils; (h) ink; (i) printing ink; (j) numbering machines.

At that time, India had a strong domestic base to manufacture all these products and used Article XVIII Section B to prevent imports of fountain pens. China's fountain pen manufacturing base in Shanghai, other than Hero, is of a later vintage. Shanghai Hero Pen Company traced its antecedents back to 1931. That is when Wolff Pen Manufacturing Company was founded, which was later renamed as Shanghai Hero Pen Company. Companies like Jinhao did not exist then. Given India's fountain pen and ink base, it was a bit strange that in 1954, it was pre-decided that China would have a comparative advantage in exporting fountain pens and ink and India would not. To reiterate, we clamped down on imports of fountain pens from the rest of the world, allowed them specifically for China and did not wish to export our own to China. If Hero pens became ubiquitous in later decades, that was not only due to smuggling through Nepal—these were legitimate imports.

## Of Courts, Cases and Customs

To convey a flavour of the times, one can quote from a
case before the Bombay High Court (A.V. Venkateswaran vs
Ramchand Sobhraj Wadhwani). This judgment delivered by the
Bombay High Court in 1961 was on appeal by the customs
department against an order of a Division Bench of the Bombay
High Court. To quote from the judgment:

> The respondent [Ramchand Sobhraj Wadhwani] carries
> on business in Bombay and he was granted on August
> 18, 1954, a licence under the Imports & Exports (Control)
> Act, 1947, for the import of fountain-pens at not less
> than Rs. 25 C.I.F. value each from soft currency area, up
> to a defined amount. He placed an order for the import
> of Sheaffer pens from Australia and a consignment of
> these was received by air in Bombay in October 1954.
> The fountain-pens thus imported had nibs which were
> gold plated and also caps and clips of similar composition.
> The question in controversy relates to the rate of duty
> to be charged on these imported pens. The Schedule
> to the Indian Tariff Act, 1934, has an item numbered
> 45(3) in relation to the article described as 'fountain pens
> complete', the rate of duty being 30 per cent., ad valorem.
> It was the case of the respondent that the imported goods
> fell within this item and were liable to be charged with duty
> at that rate. The Customs authorities, however, considered
> that the consignment fell within the description 'articles
> plated with gold or silver' being item 61(8) on which
> duty was payable at 78 per cent. The Assistant Collector
> of Customs adjudicated the duty on this latter basis and
> thereafter the respondent having filed an appeal to the

Collector of Customs, the levy was upheld by order dated February 22, 1955.[151]

Wadhwani went to court and the Bombay High Court held,

[O]n any reasonable construction of the items in the Schedule to the Indian Customs Tariff, fountain-pens did not cease to be fountain-pens because they contained parts which were plated with silver or gold and that so long as they were 'fountain-pens complete', subject to any exceptional cases of which this was not one, only duty at 30 per cent, under item 45(3) could be levied.[152]

The customs department appealed and this eventually led to the 1961 judgment, where a bench consisting of P. Gajendragadkar, A. Sarkar, K. Wanchoo, K. Dasgupta and N.R. Ayyangar upheld what the single judge had already ruled. The times were such that similar decisions by Customs authorities and consequent litigation was the norm.[153]

Today, if one reads the import and export policy documents of that period, they seem to belong to another world. Domestic manufacturing was insulated from import competition because of QRs on imports and tariffs. This extended to fountain pens and ink as well. Compared to global norms, Indian manufacturing was uncompetitive. Infant industries remained infants and never grew up. However, the country needed exports and the resultant foreign exchange to pay for essential

---

[151]'A. V. Venkateswaran, Collector Of ... vs Ramchand Sobhraj Wadhwani And ... on 4 April, 1961', Indian Kanoon, https://bit.ly/38gU1nL. Accessed on 25 May 2022.
[152]Ibid.
[153]Ibid.

imports. Exports need imported inputs too. For example, a domestically made fountain pen, to be exported, might need to import nibs or gold to make gold nibs. With a protected domestic market, where competition did not exist, this was less of a problem. However, the global export market was a competitive one. Therefore, with imports under QRs and not on OGL, a special import licence would be required to import inputs. Accordingly, an import replenishment scheme (REP) was introduced in 1966. If you were a registered exporter, a certain percentage of the value of exports would be allowed to import inputs, even if the imports of those inputs were prohibited otherwise. Accordingly, between 1988 and 1991, exporters of 'fountain/ball point pens, ball point pen refills, sign pens, fibre tip pens (all types), micro tip pens, roller-writer pens and parts thereof, and fountain pen nibs (including stainless steel fountain pen and nibs (except filter and tips of fountain pens)' were permitted to import 20 per cent of the value of imports in the form of steel balls, stainless steel coils or strips not exceeding 100 mm in width, nickel, electroplating salts and brighteners excluding sodium cyanide, cellulose acetate moulding powder, polyethylene moulding powder as packing material, ballpoint refills, clips for fountain and ballpoint pens, metal caps and barrels for pens made of gun metal, silver sterling gold-plated, effaceable types of sketch pen inks in concentrated form, nigrosine dyes and synthetic fibre tips and filters for pens.[154] For synthetic fibre tips and fillers for pens, the replenishment rate was 10 per cent, not 20 per cent. These regulations were set with reference to the

---

[154]*Import & Export Policy, April 1988-March 1991*, Vol. I, Ministry of Commerce, Government of India, 1988.

Import and Export Policy of 1988–91, announced in 1988, when some level of import liberalization had already occurred. There were import duty concessions too, as long as the product was exported. Either the duty was not paid in the first place, or it was paid and later reimbursed. Broadly speaking, since the global market was competitive and the domestic market was not necessarily so, an anti-export bias was created. To persuade uncompetitive industry to export, export subsidies were introduced. For instance, a Cash Compensatory Support (CCS) Scheme was introduced in 1966. Despite tweaking, this complicated regime continued till 1991.

Irrespective of the autarky fetter, all was not lost. One should understand that the autarky fetter was not constant over time—it became worse eventually. Towards the end of the 1950s, there was a foreign exchange crisis, which was ascribed to a liberal import licensing policy, especially of consumer goods. Therefore, stringent import controls were imposed in 1957 and the Foreign Exchange Regulation Act (FERA) permanently entered statute books. Through the Import Trade Control Policy for January–June 1957, imports were tightened and through the Import Trade Control Policy for July–September 1957, there was a virtual ban on imports of consumer goods.

There is a reason for the use of the expression 'virtual ban'. Imports of items like fountain pens were not legally banned but licences were not issued for them. In 1965, the Supreme Court ruled on a case between Joint Chief Controller of Imports and Exports, Madras, and Aminchand Mutha. Since the Aminchand Mutha firm had been dissolved, there were complicated legal issues. We will only quote the part of the judgment concerning the ban.

The last point urged was that subsequent to October 1957, Government of India changed its policy with respect to import of fountain pens with which some of the present appeals are concerned. This it was urged amounted to a ban on the import of fountain pens and it would not be open to the Joint Chief Controller to issue any licence for any period, be it January-June 1957, after the import of fountain pens had been banned from October 1957. Now there is no doubt that it is open to the Central Government under S. 3 to prohibit the import of any article but that can only be done by an order published in the official gazette by the Central Government under S. 3. The High Court has found that no such order under S. 3 of the Act has been published. Nor has any such order by the Central Government been brought to our notice. All that has been said is that in the declaration of policy—as to import, the word 'nil' appears against fountain pens. That necessarily does not amount to prohibition of import of fountain pens unless there is an order of the Central Government to that effect published in the official gazette. We therefore agree with the High Court that unless such an order is produced it would be open to the licensing authority to issue a licence for the period of January-June 1957 even after October 1, 1957.[155]

Strictly speaking, a ban had not been imposed on importing fountain pens in the late 1950s. However, import licences were

[155]"Joint Chief Controller of Imports ... vs M/S. Aminchand Mutha Etc on 21 July, 1965', IndianKanoon, https://bit.ly/3IjB0hZ. Accessed on 10 June 2022. In the quote, 'Act' refers to the Imports and Exports (Control) Act of 1947.

not being issued for pens that cost less than 25 rupees at that time.[156] If this figure is correct, looking at the prices of a dozen pens in 1963, listed in Table 1, not a single one of them would have been eligible for import. Hence, though there was no legal ban on imports, there were no imports. This was naturally good for domestic manufacturers, though not for consumers.

### Table 1: Prices of fountain pens as of 1965

| Brand name | Price in rupees per dozen | Price per pen |
|---|---|---|
| Pilot | 57–186 | 4.75–15.5 |
| Champion | 132 | 11 |
| Swan | 120 | 10 |
| Black Bird | 85.50 | 7.125 |
| Wilson | 36–66 | 3–5.5 |
| Doric | 18–72 | 1.5–6 |
| Clipper | 22–45 | 1.8–3.75 |
| Plato | 24 | 2 |
| President | 15–18 | 1.25–1.5 |

Source: The Wealth of India, Industrial Products, Part VI, Council of Scientific and Industrial Research, Delhi, 1965.

Simultaneously, in 1957, there was a ban on imports of fountain pen ink too.[157] Therefore, inks, such as Pilot, Waterman, Quink, Stephens', Parker or Swan, could no longer be imported, though they could be manufactured in India under licence. This was good for domestic brands. We have already mentioned Krishnaveni, Camlin and Sulekha. In addition, there was Harihar Research

---

[156]'Saturday Special: And Then India Scripted its Pen and Ink Story', Dr.Lamba's Awakening Call, https://bit.ly/3twuWg5. Accessed on 13 June 2022.
[157]Inputs that were required for making ink could still be imported.

Works, based in Ahmedabad and Chelpark. Bril was set up in 1964 and has been primarily manufacturing ink ever since. Over a period of time, Bril has also produced fountain pens and parts, including nibs. In the 1950s and 1960s, there were other, lesser-known and often local ink brands one heard of—Europa, Ideal, Orion, Soel, Sahi, Imperial, Victory, Samrat, Orient, Bright, Kishan, Professor, Rabbit, Nurit, Ashoka,[158] Beena, Mira, Prasad,[159] Master, Sangeeta, Nataraj,[160] Ambassador, Swink, Champion Flink, Ruby, Prabhu, Bal, Guptan, Bharat Mata, Bani, Kaka and Kakar's K. A few of these brands produced ink tablets, later metamorphosing into manufacturers of liquid ink.

## The Wealth of India

The Council of Scientific and Industrial Research (CSIR) produced a publication that was a wealth of information, appropriately titled 'The Wealth of India'. The 1965 version, just before reservations set in, has a lot of interesting information on fountain pens, nibs and ink.[161]

> The fountain pen industry had its beginning in the early thirties, but it is only during the last decade or so that it has made substantial progress. In 1964 there were 15 organized

[158]Not to be confused with the pens. This trademark for ink was registered in Rajasthan to Patodia Mombatti Works.
[159]Not to be confused with the pens. This trademark for ink was registered in Pune in 1954.
[160]Not the brand name used by Hindustan Pencils Private Limited, but a distinct ink produced by Atlas Research Industries, Madurai.
[161]*The Wealth of India, Industrial Products, Part VI*, Council of Scientific and Industrial Research, Delhi, 1965.

manufacturers of fountain pens. Two of them, namely, *Pilot Pen Co. (India) Ltd*, Madras, and *Rightaids (Orient) Pvt. Ltd*, Madras, have foreign collaboration. Other manufacturers are: *Dhiraj Pen Mfg Co.*, Bombay; *Mhatre Pen & Plastic Industries Ltd*, Bombay; *Gujarat Industries*, Bombay; *G.D.S. Chowdhury*, Delhi; *Exen Industries*, Bombay; *K.V. Ratnam & Bros*, Rajahmundry (Andhra Pradesh); *K.V. Brahmam & Sons*, Bhimavaram (Andhra Pradesh); *Jupiter Industries*, Delhi; *Prakash Metal Works*, Bombay; *Leader Fountain Pen Works*, Rajahmundry; *Zebra Instruments*, Bombay; *Asoka Pen Works*, Tenali (Andhra Pradesh); and *Seth M. B. Kapur & Co.*, Modinagar....Fountain pens are also manufactured by many small scale units in the country. In 1962, there were about 210 small units with an annual production capacity of 4,765,000 dozen pens. The statewise distribution of these units is as follows: West Bengal, 44; Maharashtra, 40; Andhra Pradesh, 31; Uttar Pradesh, 28; Madras, 25; Delhi, 17; Punjab, 13; Gujarat, 5; Rajasthan, 3; Bihar, 2; Kerala and Madhya Pradesh, 1 each [...] The total labour employed in the organized sector of the fountain pen industry is 3,000; the number employed in the small scale and cottage units in the southern zone is 330. An *ad hoc* committee of fountain pen manufacturers has been set up at the instance of the Government of India to inquire into the quality of fountain pens with a view to ascertaining and eliminating the causes leading to the production of low-grade pens.

Note that this was written before reservations and quality was an issue even then.

CSIR's publication also gives us figures on the estimated production of fountain pens between 1958 and 1963. There were yearly fluctuations but the average figure for annual production was around 10 million fountain pens. The cited production capacity of the small-scale sector (4,765,000 dozen pens) translates into 57.18 million pens a year. Even though this is production capacity and not actual quantity produced, it is still a staggering number.

Among the larger players, Pilot Pen Company, India, was, of course, the Indian subsidiary of Pilot, the Japanese pen maker, set up in Madras on 21 July 1952. Right Aids Orient was a TTK group venture, incorporated in Madras. However, its first factory was set up in 1951 in Bangalore, not in Madras, as there used to be an electricity shortage in Tamil Nadu then. Unlike Pilot Pen Company, India, Right Aids Orient was not a subsidiary. It had a licence to manufacture the Waterman brand of pens, as other Indian manufacturers would also do later. The Sanghvi brothers—Dwarakadas Jivanlal Sanghvi and Vallabhdass Jivanlal Sanghvi—with their Wilson pens were another such manufacturer. As mentioned earlier, Dhiraj Pen Manufacturing Company was set up by Vallabhdass Jivanlal Sanghvi. Mhatre Pen Plastic Industries Private Limited was established in 1951, though the antecedents go back to 1933. Mhatre also had a license to manufacture Waterman, Doric, Swan and Clipper.

There is an anecdote that one often hears. There doesn't seem to be any actual evidence for any of the elements of the said anecdote—from an American expert being invited to India to fountain pens being perceived to be consumer goods. Nonetheless, the anecdote freely circulates, establishing that one should not believe everything one reads:

In the summer of 1961, Government of India was waiting for an expert from the United States. Not an agricultural scientist or a meteorologist but someone with knowledge of the fountain pen industry. India had completely stopped importing fountain pens in 1958, and by 1960 domestic production of pens had risen to 12 million pieces in the organised sector and 10 million in cottage industries. We made enough pens for our needs—but not always to an acceptable quality. So in 1961, Government of India turned to the US for a quality control expert [...] India used to import them from the US, UK, Australia, West Germany, France, Japan, etc., but to encourage domestic manufacturing, the government had decided that pens that cost less than Rs 25 apiece would not be imported [...] But the quality of most early Indian manufacturers was iffy, so in 1956 the government approved two foreign collaborations—with Pilot and Waterman, respectively. The government hoped that the joint venture factories would make world-class pens for as little as Rs 10 apiece, but in a few years it felt the need to improve quality across the industry and called in an American technical expert.[162]

The same anecdote has been repeated in another source:

In the summer of 1961, Government of India was waiting for an expert from the United States. Not an agricultural scientist or a meteorologist but someone with knowledge of the fountain pen industry. India had completely stopped importing fountain pens in 1958, and by 1960 domestic

---

[162]'Saturday Special: And then India Scripted its Pen and Ink Story', Dr.Lamba's Awakening Call, https://bit.ly/3NDeUbU. Accessed on 25 May 2022.

production of pens had risen to 12 million pieces in the organised sector and 10 million in cottage industries. We made enough pens for our needs (although nibs were 100% imported) but always to an acceptable quality. So in 1961, Government of India turned to the US for a quality control expert [...] The government hoped that the joint venture factories would make world-class pens for as little as Rs 10 apiece, but in a few years it felt the need to improve quality across the industry and called in an American technical expert.[163]

Since fountain pens were consumer goods and the year was 1961, the story sounds implausible, although it might be true.

The questions and answer session in the Rajya Sabha on the manufacture of fountain pen ink, dated 21 May 1957, captures the flavour of the times.[164]

Shri Nawab Singh Chauhan: 'Will the Minister for Commerce and Industry be pleased to state the quantity of fountain-pen ink which is being manufactured in the country at present?'

The Deputy Minister for Commerce and Industry (Shri Satish Chandra): 'The present annual production rate of fountain pen ink, in the organized sector, is about 8 lakh dozen bottles of 2 oz. each. Production in 1956 in this sector was about 6.8 lakh

---

[163]Gaur, Abhilash, 'How India Taught Herself to Make Good Pens and Ink', *The Times of India*, 25 November 2021, https://bit.ly/3LJUsom. Accessed on 25 May 2022.

[164]All the quotes from the conversation reproduced here have been sourced from: 'Oral Answers [Rajya Sabha] to Questions', Parliament of India, Official Debates of Rajya Sabha, https://bit.ly/3xIdfMJ. Accessed on 13 June 2022.

dozen bottles. Similar information is not available in respect of Cottage Scale Units.'

Shri Manubhai Shah: 'Sir, the annual capacity of the existing units is about 35 lakh dozen bottles of 2 oz. each as against the present demand of 9 lakhs. So, the Hon. Member can appreciate that the existing rated capacity is four times the existing manufacture.'

Shri M. Valiulla: 'How many of these are manufactured by foreign companies and in how many Indians are collaborating?'

Shri Manubhai Shah: 'There are five foreign brands—the Pilot, the Watermans, the Quink, the Stephens and the Swan. Out of these, only two firms have foreign minority capital participation namely, Pilot and Quink. The others are having only foreign technical collaboration.'

Shri J.V.K. Vallabharao: 'Is it not a fact that these companies are importing ink paste and mixing it here?'

Shri Manubhai Shah: 'No. But it is true that, so far as the raw materials in the form of methylene blue and ink blue are concerned and certain proprietary ingredients are concerned, certain quantity is imported, but a large part of raw material is manufactured in the country.'

Dr Raghubir Singh: 'May I know, Sir, why all these inks are being supplied only in 2 oz. bottles and not in bigger sizes?'

Shri Manubhai Shah: 'Sir, this is a standard conversion just as 20 s. count [sic] is the conversion in textiles. It is only specified as bottles of 2 oz. size, though other sizes are also available.'

Dr Raghubir Singh: 'May I say that, so far as I know, in the market, only 2 oz. bottles are available for sale. That means an additional burden on the ordinary user of ink.'

Mr Chairman: 'That is not a question.'

Shri Kishen Chand: 'May I know from the hon. Minister if it is a fact that these foreign concerns who are manufacturing ink in India are importing small quantities of essential materials the cost of which is of a very high proportion to the cost of raw materials?'

Shri Manubahi Shah: 'Sir, it is not quite true to say that it is a very high proportion. It is a fact that certain ingredients which are of a patented type or specific type are being imported, but they bear a very small comparison to the final cost of production.'

Shri Kishen Chand: 'What is the percentage of proportion to the cost of production?'

Shri Manubhai Shah: 'It will vary from product to product. As I said all the high class ingredients having the same quality are manufactured in India today and practically, as a matter of fact, total imports are banned for the last one year of any foreign ink.'

Pandit S.S.N. Tankha: 'May I know what steps are being taken to improve the quality of the inks manufactured here so as to make them compare favourably with the foreign inks?'

Shri Manubhai Shah: 'Sir, the Tariff Commission went into this aspect very much, and I am happy to say that they found that the Indian inks like Camel, Sulekha, Harihar and Nuluk and Indian manufacture of foreign well-known brands were of excellent quality. If any Hon. Member at any time feels that any quality has deteriorated or any particular bottle is bad, and if he draws our attention to that, we will certainly look into the matter.'[165]

At that time, Pilot sold a brand named Champion. From an intellectual property rights violation case filed by Pilot, we know the brand names under which some of the Indian pens were sold. This was a bunch of cases on which the Madras High Court passed judgment in 1966.

> The plaintiff, Pilot Pen Co., claims to have absolute copy right in a new and original design in respect of fountain pen clips, having registered their design under No. 101410 dated 28-9-1959 under the Indian Patents and Designs Act 1911. It is the plaintiff's allegation that the several defendants have been manufacturing and marketing fountain pens in the name and style of Champion Registered 81 'President' and 'Mhatre Writer' respectively with clips exactly similar to or at any rate of colourable imitation of the plaintiff's registered design and have thus committed unlawful infringement and piracy of the plaintiff's design and that the several defendants have refused to comply with the plaintiffs demand to stop committing the infringement and submit accounts with regard to sale of these pens fitted with clips having the infringing design...[166]

---

[165]We have not been able to track down the brand mentioned in this quote, Nuluk, though, following the Rajya Sabha question, the name is often repeated. Nuluk may very well have been a typo for Nu-Look. Kirpal Industries, based in Indore and established in 1964, still exports the Mohni brand of fountain pen ink.

[166]'The Pilot Pen Co. (India) Private ... vs The Gujarat Industries Private ... on 21 March, 1966', IndianKanoon, https://bit.ly/3LEKqEQ. Accessed on 25 May 2022.

The judge ruled against the plaintiff's intellectual property rights being violated. One of the brands sold by Dhiraj Pen Manufacturing Company was, thus, known as President; Mhatre Pen Plastic Industries sold the Mhatre Writer and Plato; and Gujarat Industries sold under the brand name Ashok and Service. However, Mhatre sold pens under other brand names too. For example, after Eversharp was acquired by Parker Pen Company in 1957, Mhatre sold Doric, manufactured under a licence, and it also had its own brands like Writer, Homer, Commerce and Clipper. Subsequently, it also made pens for Waterman and Swan under licences. Mhatre Pen Plastic Industries, Gujarat Industries and Dhiraj Pen Manufacturing Company shut shop in the 1980s, or moved on to other products. However, Mhatre left a legacy as Ravlon.

We know what happened to Exen Industries from a case before the Supreme Court. This, too, was a case about imports, specifically import licensing. 'The facts are as follows. The appellant firm which is engaged in the manufacture of fountain pens, ball pens etc. was constituted of three partners, namely, K.N. Vora, J.L. Mehta and A.M. Bhuta. After retirement of some of the partners, the firm consisted of only two persons H.T. Vora and C.J. Mehta in November 1953.'[167] The Vohra– Mehta venture continued as Exen Industries but was dissolved in 1963. With another partner, Vora continued with Exen Industries. Mehta started making fountain pens under the name of Premier Products.

There was also a brand known as Sulekha—not to be confused with the ink or with the Sulekha brand, produced

---

[167]'Exen Industries vs The Chief Controller of Imports ... on 22 January, 1971', IndianKanoon, https://bit.ly/3Nup2U2. Accessed on 25 May 2022.

by Sulekha Works. This was an independent pen manufacturer named Sulekha, which seems to have existed, though not much information is available about it. To return to the CSIR list, we have already spoken about how K.V. Ratnam and K.V. Brahmam and Sons (Bhimavaram) were linked to K.V. Ratnam. There seems to be no record of what happened to Jupiter Industries. Prakash Metal Works still exists but has moved away from making fountain pens. There is no record of Leader Fountain Pen Works, Rajahmundry. Zebra Instruments has closed down. Asoka Pen Works, Tenali, was a small-scale unit that closed down. It used to sell Asoka brand pens, neither to be confused with Ashok pens, sold by Gujarat Industries, nor with Ashoka fountain pens and ballpoint pens, produced by Ashoka Brothers, Etawah, who also sold a fountain pen by the name of Vijay. No record seems to exist of what happened to Seth M.B. Kapoor, Modinagar, and G.D.S. Chowdhury, who were also manufacturers mentioned in *The Wealth of India* report.

## Organized Sector Production

Although CSIR is a credible source, there seem to be gaps in what has been described as 'organized' sector production of fountain pens in *The Wealth of India* report. 'Organized' is a legal term and, under the Factories Act, 1948, an enterprise is considered organized depending on whether it uses power and whether the number of employees is more or less than 10 or 20. It is doubtful that CSIR used the word 'organized' in that strict legal sense. Otherwise, Asoka Pen Works, Tenali, would not have been included in the organized sector and some others would not have been excluded from it.

The Ministry of Labour's publication for 1958 is a better source.[168] It has a category of large industrial establishments, with pens and pencils getting clubbed together. If one excludes those that are obviously connected with pencils, one has the following list: (a) Ratnam Pen Works, Rajahmundry; (b) Sastry Pen Works, Tenali; (c) Raynar Pen Works, Guntur; (d) Air Mail Pen Company, Bombay; (e) Popular Pen & Clip Industries, Bombay; (f) Dhiraj Pen Manufacturing Company, Bombay; (g) Balkrishna Pen and Plastic Manufacturing Company, Bombay; (h) Pankaj Pen Industries, Bombay; (i) National Pen Company, Bombay; (j) Venus Pen Company, Bombay; (k) Wimco Pen Company, Bombay; (l) Pilot Pen Company of India Limited, Madras; (m) Radar Fountain Pen Factory, Tiruvellore; (n) Prakash Pen, Kanpur; (o) Seth M.B. Kapoor and Company, Modinagar; and (p) Indian Pen and Allied Industries Company, Calcutta.

At that time, given the importance of manufacturing in Maharashtra, Bombay's dominance was understandable, as was Andhra Pradesh's. With this information being sourced from a publication of the labour ministry, we also have figures on the average number of workers employed. Most of the 16 enterprises listed employed less than 20 workers. With more than 200 workers, Dhiraj and Balkrishna were really large. Pilot employed around 150 and the average number employed in Kanpur and Modinagar was around 30. Balkrishna was also part of the Wilson group of companies, that is, the Sanghvi brothers. But the branding of the pens was different. Balkrishna produced Wilson, while Dhiraj produced

---

[168]India Labour Bureau, *Large Industrial Establishments in India*, Ministry of Labour and Employment, Labour Bureau, 1958.

President. National Pen Company is what exists today in the form of Flair Pen and Plastic Industries Private Limited. Wimco also has a successor in Flair, the brand it established in 1976. The Rathod family, now associated with Flair, was originally associated with Wimco. Flair is also associated with the Senator and Pentel brands. India Pen and Allied Industries, the last manufacturer mentioned in the Ministry of Labour's list, was established in 1944.

To reiterate, the CSIR list included manufacturers from 1965 and the list of the labour ministry included those from 1958. Both pre-date the 1967 small-scale industry (SSI) reservations and both miss a few other fountain-pen-making enterprises set up in the 1960s, before 1967. In 1963, there was Davindra Kumar Jain's Luxor, which introduced a fibre-tip pen in 1966 under the brand name Artist. Later, Luxor introduced several foreign brands into the Indian market—Pilot being one. This was followed by the Parker, Waterman and Papermate brands. Camlin (now Kokuyo Camlin) started making fountain pens, moving away from being just a manufacturer of ink. Deccan Pens was another manufacturer that was not mentioned in the CSIR or labour ministry lists.

Before the 1967 reservations, there were, thus, different categories of fountain pen makers: (a) foreign ones, like Pilot; (b) very large Indian units, like Dhiraj and Balkrishna; (c) large Indian manufacturers ('large' in the sense of being under the purview of the Factories Act); (d) small manufacturers, without SSI reservations being necessary; and (e) sellers who did not actually make pens but sourced their products from outside and sold them under their own brand names. Benefitting from protection from imports, the spread of education and increased demand, these fountain pen makers thrived and coexisted.

Table 1 (page 103) gives us an idea of how much these fountain pens sold for in 1963.[169] The prices mentioned in the table were wholesale prices, per dozen fountain pens. Sometimes, there was a range because the model and the quality of the nib (gold versus steel) differed.

Different companies and brands coexisted in different slices of the market. 'The popular brands of fountain pens being manufactured are: Pilot, Waterman, Wilson, Lux, Dodge, President, Olympic, Liberty, Parle, Homer, Plato, Hunter, Doric, Champion, Ashok and Mayor.'[170] In addition, 'Only costly pens [were] imported.' Given the import restrictions, this was understandable. Indeed, given the import restrictions, it was odd that fountain pens were imported at all. Imports dramatically dropped from 2,428 pens in 1960–61 to eight in 1962–63. In 1962–63, the average cost of an imported pen was 17 rupees. For a dozen of these, the expense would have been 208 rupees, far more than the most expensive 14 karat gold pens produced in India. The cost of the imported pens naturally included import duties. With severe import restrictions, smuggling was inevitable. In later years, this happened via Nepal. In the initial years, smuggling was common through former French or Portuguese territories. The sharp drop in imports after 1961 was probably because of import restrictions

---

[169]Collated from *The Wealth of India, Industrial Products*, Part VI, Council of Scientific and Industrial Research, Delhi, 1965.

[170]Ibid. Some of these brands are difficult to pin down now. Lux was probably a Waterman brand, Dodge was probably a Graf von Faber-Castell brand, Olympic was a local Indian brand, Liberty was probably from Cross, Parle must have been a local Indian brand. Many of these may have been local Indian brands.

but may also have had something to do with Goa becoming part of the Union of India in 1961. Oddly, exports of fountain pens also dropped sharply from 610,258 pens in 1960–61 to 358,515 pens in 1962–63. Even more oddly, these exports of fountain pens happened for less than one rupee a piece, which was partly explained by export subsidies[171] because export prices make it easier to quote lower global prices than otherwise.

Other than the ones mentioned above, several other fountain pen manufacturers and their long-lost brands remain only as names now with most details missing.[172]

**Nibs for Writing**

Before concluding this chapter, one would also like to mention nibs. 'Gold nibs used in fountain pens are produced by *Pilot Pen Co. (India) Pvt. Ltd.*, Madras; *Rightaids (Orient) Pvt. Ltd*, Madras; *K.V. Ratnam & Bros*, Rajahmundry; *Leader Fountain Pen Works*, Rajahmundry; and *K.V. Brahmam & Sons*, Bhimavaram. Gold-plated stainless steel nibs are manufactured by 9 organized manufacturers of fountain pens and 13 small units in Sattur (Madras State).'[173] The CSIR listing does not mention Ambitious Gold Nib Manufacturing Company, set up a little later, in 1965, though Ambitious was registered as a fountain pen and nib trademark in 1960 in Delhi. From 1958 to 1963, the gold nibs produced were limited in number. Most

---

[171] *The Wealth of India, Industrial Products*, Part VI, Council of Scientific and Industrial Research, Delhi, 1965.

[172] Please see Appendix I for a detailed list.

[173] *The Wealth of India*, Industrial Products, Part VI, Council of Scientific and Industrial Research, Delhi, 1965.

nibs produced were made out of steel. Gold-plated iridium or steel nibs were roughly half the number of steel nibs produced. A very small number of nibs were imported and exported.

Sattur was a major centre for making fountain pen nibs, though these were small-scale family businesses—cottage industries, so to speak. Since most of these businesses were small-scale, robust figures are difficult to get. But there seem to have been around 250 enterprises making fountain pen nibs in Sattur alone, with steel imported from the US and the Soviet Union. These are figures from the 1960s, when Sattur had a large market share of nibs manufactured domestically. However, a similar figure is also cited for the 1980s. But that was a long time ago. Today, the number has dropped dramatically. Sattur has been important enough for dissertations to be written on the place. One such dissertation, authored in 2013, mentioned 53 nib-making units in Sattur, though the number may have declined further since then. It also tells us that Thiru Rajagopalasari migrated from Kerala and set up the first nib-making unit in Sattur in 1941.[174] Like Sattur, at some point, Thanjavur was famous for nibs—the ones meant for calligraphy. While discussing calligraphy, one should mention Mehra Leonardt Pens Private Limited, incorporated in Bombay in 1958, with antecedents that go back to 1930.[175] This was

---

[174]Thangraj, K., *The Problems and Prospects of Fountain Pen Nib Industrial Units in Sattur block of Virudhunagar District, Tamil Nadu*, Ph.D. dissertation, Madurai Kamaraj University, 2013.
[175]The original Leonardt and Company (established in 1856) now exists in the form of Manuscript Pen Company. B.N. Mehra and Company was established in Delhi in 1930 by three brothers, Baij Nath Mehra, Amar Nath Mehra and Ram Nath Mehra. It dealt in paper and stationery and then started to import fountain pens and associated products. Mehra

an Indo-British enterprise, specializing in the manufacture of dip pen nibs, with brands like Kita, G-Pen, Amar Jyoti and Ambassador.

Despite the autarky fetters described in this chapter, the 1950s and 1960s were a good period for fountain pen manufacturing and the production of its parts. Fountain pens are not made in isolation—they require a manufacturing and industrial base. They require the creation of ancillary industries. All these were steadily developed during this period. In terms of vintage, there were two generations of manufacturers— pre-Independence and those set up in the 1950s and 1960s. Plus, there was a Pilot subsidiary from 1952. Before domestic fetters were superimposed on the autarky fetter, there were several players, with quite a bit of action. The Indian Fountain Pen Manufacturers' Association was also established in 1954. However, it is a relatively dormant organization now, compared to the more active and local Bombay Fountain Pen Manufacturers & Traders Association, established in 1968 and now renamed to the Pen and Stationery Association of India.[176]

---

Leonardt Private Limited was set up to manufacture nibs and has now shut shop. But the Mehra family also established Hindustan Pencils Private Limited, which still exists.

[176]There are other associations too, like the Delhi Pen Dealers' and Manufacturers' Association, the Tamil Nadu Pen Manufacturers and Dealers Association, the Vidarbha Pen and Stationers Association and the Indian chapter of the Writing Instruments Manufacturers Organisation.

# 6

# DOMESTIC FETTERS: THE UNMAKE OF THE 1970s AND 1980s

Fountain pens, ones that university students use for writing, you know, were in short supply. The participants asked the director of a fountain pen plant why he had not produced fountain pens. He replied that he had not been supplied with metallurgical materials. They asked the director of a steel mill why he had failed to supply the fountain pen plant with materials. He said: Because I did not get any iron ore from the smelter. The director of the smelter said that he had not gotten ore from the mine. The responsible official at the mine said: I produced some, but rail transportation was not available to the smelter. The railways minister was then summoned and asked: Why did you not transport the mineral ore? He said: Because we did not get any railroad ties from the Forestry Ministry. The Forestry Ministry replied that it did not have any gas to produce timber. [177]

---

[177]Cited in, Oh, Kongdan and Ralph C. Hassig, *North Korea through the Looking Glass,* Brookings Institution Press, 2000.

No, this is not a description of India. It is a description of North Korea and the quoted text is from a meeting of the State Administrative Council in 1988 to discuss fountain pens. Classic centrally planned economies have depended on central allocation of resources, implying centralized decision-making about production, distribution and consumption. This allocative function has never been performed efficiently and there are several instances to illustrate how such planning led to disasters. India was never as centralized as North Korea, and former centrally planned economies have moved away from historical excesses. However, in the heyday of planning in India, in the 1950s, 1960s and 1970s, there were excesses too. Consequently, competition, choice and quality suffered.

At least so far as fountain pens and fountain pen inks are concerned, from the late 1960s to the early 1980s, India did not become a shortage economy. But it was an economy where quality suffered and fountain pens became more fountains and less pens. The autarky fetter led to competition from abroad being prevented. The domestic fetters, which will be discussed in this chapter, led to domestic protection being curtailed. It was a protected, profitable and uncompetitive market. Quality was bound to suffer.

In an overall perspective for the economy, the 1960s and the 1970s are sometimes described as lost development decades for India. It was no different for fountain pens and allied industries, though this chapter details the 1970s and 1980s. Ostensibly, these sectors did well, oblivious of the fact that, one day, there would be competition, the absence of protection and a technological shock. The rest of the world did change. Four examples will illustrate this.

First, Lamy, the German fountain pen and writing

instrument manufacturer, originated in 1930, when a pen manufacturer named Orthos was bought over by Josef Lamy. However, the company moved to a completely different trajectory in 1966, when the Lamy design that everyone is familiar with today was conceived. Its marketing and distribution changes came after that. Second, Scrikss, originally a Spanish brand, was sold to a Turkish businessman in 1963. The first Scrikss factory was established in Turkey in 1964 and foreign collaborations and improvements in technology ensued. Third, the Wolff Pen Manufacturing Company, established in Shanghai in 1931, became the Shanghai Hero Pen Company in 1966. By then, it had also become a state-owned company. Wolff Pen Manufacturing Company represented private foreign investments. After the Great Leap Forward in 1958 and the consequent nationalistic fervour, Shanghai Hero consciously sought to catch up with Parker and this led to Hero's great expansion. As a pen manufacturer, TWSBI (the name means 'Hall of Three Cultures') was formed in 2009 and has been a well-regarded Taiwanese brand. However, it started manufacturing fountain pens later. The antecedents of TWSBI (without the BI, which stands for writing instruments) as an original equipment manufacturer (OEM) go back to the 1960s.

Three of the countries that these manufacturers belong to—China, Turkey and Taiwan—are not traditional fountain pen manufacturers. One is not talking about Europe and North America. These three countries invested in technology and exported fountain pens, which were regarded as consumer goods. Elsewhere in East Asia, in other segments, countries became exporters of consumer goods, which are labour-intensive in production. There is a global market for such goods. In contrast, in India, consumer goods were regarded as luxury items, those that were not quite necessary. If domestic production was frowned upon, there would be no competitive exports either. The basis of Indian planning was an emphasis on capital goods, not consumer goods. Not only did choice and competition suffer domestically but India also failed to tap into export markets, which would have ensured employment as well.

## Domestic Restraints: Regulation and Policy

In India, fountain pens suffered because of domestic fetters in the form of policy-induced distortions. The domestic fetters took the form of reservations for the small-scale sector, a clamping down on large-scale industry, labour laws and exchange controls that worked against foreign direct investments (FDI). It could, of course, have been worse, as consumer goods, fountain pens and fountain pen inks were not reserved for production by the public sector. Had that been the case, like watches, HMT would have ended up producing Janata fountain pens and Janata fountain pen ink. There would have been a shortage of pens and, like watches before liberalization, Members of Parliament would have had a discretionary quota for Janata fountain pens and Janata fountain pen ink. However, there were no shortages of pens and their quantity did not suffer, but their quality did.

The statutory powers for small-scale sector reservations came through the IDRA, 1951. This statement is only partly true. The IDRA, 1951, gave the government the powers to introduce industrial licensing. Until the IDRA was amended in 1984, the government did not possess any statutory powers for small-scale sector reservations. However, no one ever challenged small-scale sector reservations in court. The best introduction to the policy of reservations was written by the now-forgotten Abid Hussain Committee.

> The policy of reservation was primarily initiated in 1967 as a promotional and protective measure for the small-scale sector vis-à-vis the large-scale sector. Under this policy selected products are identified for exclusive production in the small-scale sector [...] No new unit in medium or large-scale sector is allowed to be set up after the date of reservation, nor any further capacity expansion in the existing medium or large-scale units is permitted. All further expansion or capacity creations reserved for the small-scale sector [...] The medium or large-scale industrial units can continue to manufacture reserved items in cases as mentioned below:
>
> a. The existing medium or large unit which had already been manufacturing an item when it is put on the reserved list. In such a case the unit has to obtain a Carry on Business (COB) Licence from the Ministry of Industry. The capacity of the unit is pegged at the highest production level achieved by the unit in the last three years preceding the date of reservation of the product.
>
> b. If the existing SSI units manufacturing reserved items graduate by their process of growth into medium/ large scale, such have to obtain a COB Licence wherein the capacity is pegged with respect to the date when it became incumbent on the unit to apply for and obtain on the unit to apply for and obtain a COB Licence [...]

The Industries Development and Regulation Act, 1951 has been amended in 1984 to give statutory backing to the policy of reservation empowering the government to reserve selected items for production by the ancillary or small-scale industrial undertaking. The amendment also provided that the central government would constitute an Advisory Committee with a view to determining the nature of any article or classes of articles that may be reserved for production by the ancillary or small-scale industrial undertaking.[178]

Even though the statutory powers did not exist, reservations for the SSI sector were introduced in 1967. Until this happened, one did not form the impression that 'unmake in India' was going to happen for fountain pens. A valid argument can, of course, be made about the absence of import competition, but the first nail in the coffin was SSI reservations. As the quote from the Abid Hussain Committee's Report indicates, reservations cut off domestic competition. Production by non-SSI enterprises was frozen at the existing level, preventing further expansion. New entry into the sector would have to be from SSI. The Industrial Policy Resolution of 1948 also recognized the possible importance of SSI, including from the point of view of ensuring employment and countering artificially high capital intensity of production.

Prior to introducing reservations in 1967, there were fiscal concessions in favour of SSI, which distorted resource allocation. However, reservations prevented competition.

---

[178]'Report of the Expert Committee on Small Enterprises', Development Commission, Ministry of Micro, Small & Medium Enterprises, 1997, https://bit.ly/3HiIHEH. Accessed on 13 June 2022.

Moreover, the definition of SSI was fixed in nominal terms (investments in plant and machinery) and this was not recalibrated to keep pace with inflation, distorting the bias even more towards the small. Table 2, reproduced from the Abid Hussain Committee Report, indicates the progressive increase in the number of items reserved for SSI. Since the National Industrial Classification (NIC) codes have changed, one should be careful in interpreting the increase in number of items reserved. For example, the jump in 1978 was entirely because of the new codes. However, it is also true that the peak of reservations came about in 1984.

Table 2: Progressive increase in reservations

| Date of Notification | No. of items reserved | No. of items deserved | Cumulative net number of items reserved |
|---|---|---|---|
| **Phase 1** | **47** | | **47** |
| 1 April 1967 | 8 | | 55 |
| 19 Feb 1970 | 73 | | 128 |
| 24 Feb 1971 | | 4 | 124 |
| 11 Nov 1971 | | | 177 |
| 26 Feb 1974 | 53 | | 180 |
| 5 June 1976 | 3 | | 504 |
| 26 April 1978 | 324 | | |
| **Phase II** | | | **807** |
| 26 April 1978 | 807 | | 806 |
| 30 Dec 1978 | | 1 | 833 |
| 12 May 1980 | 27 | | 833 |

| 19 Feb 1981 | 1 | 1 | 842 |
|---|---|---|---|
| 3 Aug 1981 | 9 | | 831 |
| 23 Dec 1981 | 2 | 13 | 282 |
| 14 Oct 1982 | | 3 | 837 |
| 19 Oct 1982 | 9 | | 872 |
| 3 Sept 1983 | 35 | | 873 |
| 18 Oct 1981 | 1 | 1 | 869 |
| 30 May 1984 | 7 | 14 | 863 |
| 13 Feb 1987 | 1 | 7 | 850 |
| 20 July 1987 | | 13 | 847 |
| 18 Mar 1988 | | 3 | 846 |
| 3 Mar 1989 | 3 | 1 | 835 |
| 31 July 1989 | 1 | 14 | 836 |

*Source:* 'Report of the Expert Committee on Small Enterprises', Development Commission, Ministry of Micro, Small & Medium Enterprises, 1997, https://bit.ly/3HiIHEH. Accessed on 13 June 2022.

## Reservation: The Rationale or Lack Thereof

In principle, an economic case can be made for reservation. However, how and why were items singled out for reservation? Having examined various criteria, the Abid Hussain Committee concluded the following:

> The last point suggests a reason why we have no explanation in official documents anywhere how the list of reserved items have been selected, and on what basis additional items have been added. The changes over time gives the impression that the choice of products

was somewhat arbitrary. Eighty percent of the reserved items are concentrated in 11 three-digit NIC categories. The remainder are spread over 90 three-digit categories. This heavy concentration of policy incidence, together with a long tail demonstrates, to some extent, successful lobbying for reservation by special interest groups. In the absence of a well-defined and rational criterion for product selection—which, we have suggested, is impossible in practice—the scope for such action remains large, and its potential for welfare loss to the consumers and the economy increases commensurably.[179]

Stated simply, decisions were either ad hoc or influenced by lobbying. Despite tomes having been written on the history of economic policymaking in India, no one seems to have answered two questions.

1.  Who took the reservation decision? SSI reservations occurred at the time of the Second Five Year Plan (1956–61), not the First Five Year Plan (1951–56), and the intellectual support was provided by the 1955 Karve Committee.[180] However, the First Five Year Plan, the Second Five Year Plan, the Third Five Year Plan (1961–66) and the Karve Committee talked about policies to support SSI, not reservations. The Karve Committee talked of purchase preference from SSI and support for technological upgradation, but it did not mention reservations or even price preferences

---

[179]Ibid.

[180]'Report of the Village and Small Scale Industries (Second Five Year Plan) Committee', Government of India Press, New Delhi, 1955.

for purchases from SSI. Reservations were actually introduced during the Plan Holiday, in between the Third Five Year Plan and the Fourth Five Year Plan (1969–74). So, we have no satisfactory explanation of who decided to introduce SSI reservations in 1967.

2. Who drew up the original list of 47 items? So far as reservations are concerned, the intellectual support was provided not by the Karve Committee, despite being blamed for this, but by the Hazari and Dutt committees.

Rather intriguingly, fountain pens were in the initial list of 47 items to be reserved in 1967. This prevented large enterprises from making a fresh entry into the sector and, since existing large enterprises were not asked to close down (when reservations were introduced), it cushioned them against competition. Could there have been lobbying by existing fountain pen manufacturers for reservations since this was one of the reasons cited by the Abid Hussain Committee for the selection of items for reservations? This does not sound very plausible, though it was not impossible. As the description of earlier chapters shows, in addition to a cottage industry of fountain pen makers, there were large industrial establishments that made pens along with a few very large ones. It is certainly possible that they lobbied against fresh entry and competition. However, in all probability, the other reason mentioned by the Abid Hussain Committee is the real one behind including fountain pens on the original list of 47 reserved goods—it was a completely arbitrary and ad hoc exercise. Simply because fountain pens happened to be regarded as consumer goods, they were reserved.

After the Micro, Small and Medium Enterprises Development Act of 2006, the SSI nomenclature has, of course, been overtaken. There has indeed been liberalization. First, definitions of SSI/MSME have been broadened. Second, with an equity limit, FDI is permitted in the SSI sector. Third, large enterprises can also invest in SSI. Fourth, reservations for fountain pens, parts and ink have gone, progressively and in degrees. But that historical reservation has left a legacy. India is not exceptional in possessing the SSI legacy, not even for fountain pens. Along with the GATT negotiations, in 1951, there was the Trade Agreements Extension Act in the US, authorizing the US president to enter into bilateral or regional trade negotiations and agreements. The views of the American fountain pen industry were submitted before the US Senate.

> For a considerable time before the Tariff Act of 1922 and up to the disruption of foreign trade by the Second World War (1939), Japan was consistently and overwhelmingly the principal supplier of imported fountain pens [...] Because of the constantly widening gap in production costs and the increasing competitive advantage enjoyed by Japanese producers over American producers, the domestic pen manufacturers believe that any adjustment in these tariff rates should be upward [...] The American fountain-pen industry includes 184 producing companies and is characterized by small-business producers widely distributed throughout the United States. The great bulk of these 184 producing companies make the lower-retail-priced fountain pens ($1 and less) which constitute the greatest volume of American production and American consumption (75 per cent).[181]

---

[181] *Trade Agreements Extension Act of 1951, Hearings before the Committee on Finance*, United States Government Printing Office, Washington, 1951.

In other words, (a) the US fountain pen industry was also characterized by small-scale production and (b) there were 184 such manufacturers.

Protectionist pressures are universal across countries. Competition implies free entry and exit. Faced with this competition, inefficient enterprises close down and capital moves to sectors where its productivity is greater. While small may be beautiful, beauty does not always have much to do with business and commercial decision-making. There are economies of scale and scope, not only in production but also in marketing and distribution. Ipso facto, the number of small-scale producers is not a yardstick for success. In the increasingly complicated and inter-connected world of business, it is difficult to decide what an 'American' fountain pen is, just as it is difficult to determine what an 'Indian' fountain pen is. Most American fountain pen brands perceived as such are no longer American in any way. Few manufacture pens themselves. The brands are American, but they outsource the entire production. This is true of Monteverde, Sheaffer, Conklin or the Metropolitan Museum of Art. Whatever be the definition of American, 184 fountain pen manufacturers do not exist in the US today. That is not only because of competition but also because the nature of the writing instrument market has changed. In a similar vein, there is no reason to lament the closure of manufacturers who historically made fountain pens in India. It becomes a cause for lamentation only when the number of producers dwindles to no more than a few. In every sphere of manufacturing, there are economies of scale in production and marketing. Small is not necessarily beautiful in business.

## Against Large-Scale Enterprise

The second example of a domestic fetter was the general clamping down on large-scale industry. The intellectual support for this was provided by the Monopolies Inquiry Commission, 1965, the Hazari Committee, 1967, and the Dutt Committee, 1969. All three underlined the lack of transparency in industrial licensing and problems in the way licences were issued. The Hazari Committee recommended, 'As a matter of policy, Government should declare that certain traditional industrial activities shall be closed in future to the specified ten or fifteen largest industrial houses and their associates. This would imply that the large houses already established in these activities shall not be permitted to expand in these areas, which would henceforth be reserved for small houses and independent businessmen.'[182] The Dutt Committee recommended,

> The growth of small and medium industries could be encouraged through the licensing system only in areas where reservations for certain products or processes could be successfully enforced at an appropriate stage of development of the concerned industries, and these were accompanied by supporting measures such as technical, financial and marketing assistance [...] From the time of the Karve Committee's Report, it has been envisaged that after a certain period of protection, with proper technical guidance and the development of financial and marketing facilities, units in this sector should be able to withstand competition from large scale units. Therefore, the reservations would

---

[182]Hazari, R.K., 'Industrial Planning and Licensing Policy: Final Report', Planning Commission, Government of India, 1967.

be temporary. The D.C.S.S.I. continues to work out lists of areas where such reservations are recommended by it; and these are examined by Government and decisions on reservations and bans are taken.[183]

The Monopolies Inquiry Commission, 1965, did not think that fountain pens and fountain pen ink were worth considering. It did examine pencils and concluded the degree of concentration in pencils was low.[184] And it stated,

> The production of small-scale industries has been of some importance in combating the effect of concentration in certain industries [...] It appears to use that the Government is fully conscious of the importance of helping the growth of small scale industries. Various steps have already been taken for that purpose and others are being contemplated as a result of the recommendations of the Lokanathan Committee and other Committees. It is therefore unnecessary for us to make any special recommendation in this respect.'[185]

Incidentally, the Lokanathan Committee, 1965, neither examined fountain pens nor fountain pen ink. It did not

---

[183]Dutt, S., 'Report of the Industrial Licensing Policy Inquiry Committee', Ministry of Industrial Development, Government of India, 1969. In this quote, D.C.S.S.I. stands for development commissioner for small-scale industries.

[184]'Report of the Monopolies Inquiry Commission, 1965, Volumes I and II', Government of India, New Delhi, 1965. For pencils, the share of the top three enterprises was 54.2 per cent.

[185]'Report of the Monopolies Inquiry Commission, 1965, Volumes I and II', Government of India, New Delhi, 1965.

recommend reservations either.[186]

By the time it came to the Industrial Policy Resolution of 1977, reservations for SSI were firmly in place.

> The emphasis of industrial policy so far has been mainly on large industries neglecting cottage industries completely relegating small industries to a minor role. It is the firm policy of this Government to change this approach [...] It is the policy of the Government that whatever can be produced by small and cottage industries must only be so produced [...] For this purpose an exhaustive analysis of industrial products, has been made to identify those items which are capable of being established or expanded in the small scale sector. This list of industries which would be exclusively reserved for the small-scale sector has been significantly expanded and will now include more than 500 items as compared to about 180 items earlier.[187]

We are still none the wiser about (a) who decided to reserve; (b) how were the items chosen; and (c) why fountain pens were included. All that we know from these quotes is that this was done by the Development Commissioner for Small Scale Industries, suggesting it was arbitrary and ad hoc. Thus, fountain pens were reserved for SSI. The combined

[186]Lokanathan, P.S., 'Committee on Scarce Raw Materials: Report', Ministry of Industry and Supply, Government of India Press, New Delhi, 1965.
[187]'India's Industrial Policies From 1948 To 1991', *Eastern Economist*, Vol. 70, 1978, Internet Archive, https://bit.ly/3mPQKj2. Accessed on 15 June 2022.

impact of these committees, especially the Monopolies Inquiry Commission, was the Monopolies and Restrictive Trade Practices Act (MRTP) of 1969, reflecting the general clamping down on large-scale industry. As mentioned earlier, 'large' enterprises that manufactured fountain pens existed. Reservations froze their production capacities at the existing levels and prevented upgradation of technology. The anti-large mindset made them unwelcome.

## Against Foreign Exchange

The third domestic fetter was the FERA, 1973, a more draconian piece of legislation than its antecedent, the FERA of 1947. The FERA 1947 owed its origins to wartime shortages and the Defence of India Act, 1939, though it became a part of the permanent set of statutes. There were several arguments that suggested FERA of 1947 be tightened up. For instance, a 1972 report of the Law Commission[188] and a 1971 study team chaired by M.G. Kaul to examine leakages through foreign exchange manipulation. Suffice to say, FERA, 1973 was passed and included sections (repealed through an amendment in 1993) requiring dilution in equity to 40 per cent. Equity over 40 per cent required specific approval from the Reserve Bank of India (RBI) and diversification. This led to high profile exits, like IBM and Coca Cola, while Hindustan Lever chose to diversify. Fountain pens figured in the consumer goods category, where

---

[188]'Law Commission of India, Forty-Seventh Report on The Trial and Punishment of Social and Economic Offences', Law Commission of India, Government of India, 1972, https://bit.ly/3wRpg0G. Accessed on 25 May 2022.

FDI was not deemed essential. FERA, 1973 required existing foreign enterprises to dilute equity, with exceptions to the cap only being allowed under specific cases. This led to complicated procedures and deterred future entry. 'Fifty-four companies applied to exit India by 1977–1978 and nine companies applied to exit in 1980–1981.'[189]

One thinks of FERA, 1973, only in terms of what it did to existing 'foreign' companies. Its negative impact was no less serious for possible future entrants. While the closure of Pilot Pen Company (India) in 1978 could not be directly attributed to FERA alone, since there were labour problems too, FERA did deter other possible entry of foreign brands.

## Labour and Laws

Stated simply, in the 1970s, 'imports', 'foreign' and 'large' were all undesirable and small was beautiful. The fourth domestic fetter was Chapter V-B of the Industrial Disputes Act enacted in 1947. It introduced rigidities in the organized labour market. This included the part of the labour market that was under the purview of the Industrial Disputes Act—enterprises that were covered by the Factories Act of 1948. For example, Section 9A of the Industrial Disputes Act made technological upgradation extremely difficult. Additional rigidities crept in over time. Chapter V, on strikes and lock-outs, existed in the original piece of legislation. But Chapter V-A, on lay-offs and retrenchment, was inserted in 1964, while Chapter V-B was inserted in 1976.

---

[189]Choudhury, Prithwiraj and Tarun Khanna, 'Charting Dynamic Trajectories: Multinational Enterprises in India', *Business History Review*, Vol. 88, No. 1, 2014, pp. 133–169., doi:10.1017/S000768051300144X.

The latter had special provisions on 'lay-off, retrenchment and closure in certain establishments.'[190] Stated simply, if the number of employees was more than hundred, Chapter V-B required permission from the 'appropriate government' before lay-offs, retrenchment and closure. Chapter V-A also had similar provisions, but instead of requiring the permission of the appropriate government, only a notification was required.

Along with the Industrial Disputes Act, there was also a broader tightening up of labour laws and their implementation. Beyond statutes, the general labour climate was another factor—unionism and labour unrests plagued the larger manufacturers. This was especially true of West Bengal and Maharashtra. As mentioned earlier, Sulekha closed down because of such labour problems. In Maharashtra, such issues also plagued Kiron and Company and Dhiraj Pen Manufacturing Company, which faced their first strike in 1961–62. In an attempt to fragment production and remain outside the ambit of labour laws, Balkrishna Pen Private Limited, and later, Eversharp Pen Company Private Limited, were formed. Balkrishna Pen Private Limited converted to Balkrishna Pen Export Company in 1987. These were offshoots of Dhiraj Pen Manufacturing Company. This did not help matters. Indeed, a case in Bombay High Court entered legal textbooks for determining whether a strike that commenced before the end of the notice period was legal or not.[191] The

---

[190]Gajjar, Krupa, 'Special Provisions Relating to Lay-Off, Retrenchment and Closure Under Industrial Disputes Act', Legal Service India E-Journal, https://bit.ly/3yTnFKF. Accessed on 25 May 2022.

[191]'Maharashtra General Kamgar Union ... vs Balkrishna Pen Pvt. Ltd. And ... on 10 September, 1987', IndianKanoon, https://bit.ly/3NBzMQM. Accessed on 25 May 2022.

succession of strikes crippled enterprises, especially because the bulk of the competition, with outsourced production, was outside the ambit of labour laws. Under the rigidity of labour laws, the Factories Act only became applicable if there were at least 10 employees with the use of power or 20 employees without the use of power. Therefore, to circumvent labour laws, companies fragmented production. This adversely affected quality. Therefore, there were temporary closures, followed by permanent closures.

## Ballpoints and a Shrinking Market

Despite the protected market and autarky and domestic fetters, the milieu of the time was not conducive for fountain pens. There was an onslaught of ballpoint pens.

> The manufacture of ballpoint pens started even later, although a foreign maker of 'Biro' pens had offered to set up a factory as early as 1953. The government had rejected that offer because the company wanted 49% stake in the joint venture and a high percentage of royalty. The first approval to make ballpoint pen ink in India was granted in 1962 for a joint venture between Dhirajlal Mohanlal Joshi, a businessman based in Rajkot, Gujarat, and M/s Formulabs Inc of Escondido, California [...] Today, banks recommend that you sign cheques with a ballpoint to prevent fraud, but back in the 1960s ballpoint pens were not allowed for many uses in India. You could fill out a money order with a ballpoint but the payee had to sign with a fountain pen. Bills, government cheques

and endorsements made on government cheques all had
to be with fountain pens.[192]

'Biro' had become a generic term for ballpoint pens, after the
name of Laszlo Biro. In all probability, that offer in 1953 would
have come from Eversharp, Reynolds or Parker, though it could
have come from Société Bic too. The reference in the quote is to
Joshi-Formulabs Private Limited, owner of the brand 'Easyrite'.
Why 1962? Because that is the time the writing of cheques
with ballpoint pens became acceptable. Over a period of time,
government and legal documents and examinations came to
accept ballpoint pens, which were more convenient.

The ballpoint pen was not the first or the only technological
advancement. What is a fountain pen and what distinguishes it
from a dip pen? In Chapter 2, we gave a complicated definition
of a fountain pen, as per the *Hutton's Mathematical Dictionary*.
Unlike a dip pen, which requires an inkpot to fill ink, a fountain
pen has a reservoir to store ink inside the pen. Compared
to a dip pen, a fountain pen makes writing convenient. The
quality of writing does not depend only on the fountain pen
as a writing instrument but also on the quality of paper and
of ink. A fountain pen has: (a) a reservoir for storing ink;
(b) a nib; (c) a feed that connects the nib to the reservoir,
with grooves (the collector) that control the flow of excess ink;
(d) a cap, with or without a clip; and (e) a barrel. There have
been improvements in each of these over time.

Most initial fountain pens were eyedroppers. The barrel
itself stored the ink, filled with a dropper. Unlike other filling

---

[192]Gaur, Abhilash, 'How India Taught Herself to Make Good Pens and
Ink', *The Times of India*, 25 November 2021, https://bit.ly/3LJUsom.
Accessed on 25 May 2022.

mechanisms, an eyedropper pen can store an enormous amount of ink. But how much of an advantage is this? How much does one write these days? One is liable to stain one's hands while filling the ink. If the threads that connect the section (the nib and the feed assembled) to the barrel are imperfect in any way, the pen will leak. In the heyday of fountain pen usage, the frequency of air travel was lower. So, the problem of the change in air pressure during air travel making the pen leak was not as prominent. On the other hand, when on the ground and not in the air, if the fountain pen is not full, an eyedropper pen will often burp out ink, again because of that difference in air pressure (too much of ink oozes out when there is a variation of pressure, such as on airplanes or when the level of ink in the reservoir declines).

Other than an onslaught of ball pens, technology around the reservoir also changed, especially since the 1970s. From eye dropper pens, technology moved to converters or other suction mechanisms and cartridges. The material for the body moved from ebonite to acrylic, which was much more attractive. However, such technology came at a cost. If one constrains the necessary process that came with it by artificially favouring the small-scale, one is reduced to the wisecrack about fountain pens being more fountains and less pens. While India was never North Korea, both economies shared the characteristics of shortage economies. Import competition was ruled out. Domestic protection was precluded. Therefore, when the economy opened up post-1991 and consumers benefitted from choice, inefficient domestic production was bound to exit.

## Prolific Decades, Despite Restrictions

All of this came later. In the 1970s and 1980s, insulated from competition, there was quite a bit of action. As one collates from the MCA database, there is a fairly long list of firms and brands from that time. Several of them were dealers and not manufacturers, and they often dealt in ballpoint pens and other stationery products, not just fountain pens. In addition, these companies were not completely independent, though no corporate governance norms needed to be violated because of this. Indeed, as we have documented earlier, the Sanghvi family has a long history of being associated with pen manufacturing. For instance, 'Ashok Dwarkadas Sanghvi is a director registered with MCA with DIN 1501566 Number. He or She is registered in a total of 18 companies/LLP.'[193]

From the MCA database, we have a list of the following firms.

- Awa Pens Private Limited, Kanpur
- Balaji Pens Private Limited, Bombay
- Bedi Stores, Calcutta, with brands like Guru, Banker and Rocky
- Best Pens Private Limited, Madras/Pondicherry
- Crown Pen Company Private Limited, Bombay
- Cute Pens Private Limited, Ludhiana
- Eversharp Pen Company Private Limited, Bombay
- Fisher Pen Company, Gujarat
- Multi Pens Private Limited, Madras
- Nalanda Pen Manufacturing Company Private Limited,

---

[193]'Director Info Ashok Dwarkadas Sanghvi', AllCompanyInfo, https://bit.ly/3sRCIAE. Accessed on 25 May 2022. In the quote, LLP stands for limited liability partnership.

Ahmedabad. Nalanda Pen Manufacturing Company figured in an excise case. We will quote from the judgment to illustrate two points: (a) With changing times, pens often meant ballpoint pens, not fountain pens; (b) typically, production was outsourced to avail of small-scale sector concessions.

M/s. Nalanda Pen Mfg. Company Private Limited manufactured, among other articles, ball point pens and refills for ball point pens. One of the important part of the refills namely brass tips was got manufactured by them from seven Private Limited Companies on job work basis. The job workers were operating as Small Sector Industries. They were also buying such tips on outright basis from another manufacturer. M/s. Nalanda Pen Mfg. Co. Pvt. Ltd., were filing classification lists from time to time. The job workers in the Small Sector Industries were exempted from licencing control having filed the requisite declarations from time to time in which the goods manufactured were declared as 'Brass tips of the ball point pens' and benefit of Notification No. 74/86 as amended by another notification was claimed for their duty-free clearances.[194]

The rest of the judgment does not concern us, though the contention (dismissed by the court) was about deliberate fragmentation of production.

---

[194]'Nalanda Pen Mfg. Co. Pvt. Ltd. vs Collector of C. Ex. on 31 December, 1997', IndianKanoon, https://bit.ly/3LKyX6E. Accessed on 13 June 2022.

- Rebnok Pens Private Limited, Mumbai. The Rebnok website states:

  In 1970's when European & Japanese technology was ruling the global writing instruments industry, we started our journey with a very small back room setup while focusing and giving importance to quality & design originality [...] Great care has been taken to develop high quality moulds from Korea, Taiwan & Japan to maintain product quality [...] Our in-house facility consists of refill machines, pad & screen printing machines, foiling machines, and most importantly top of the line German & Japanese injection moulding machines to produce great design & quality products.[195]

  However, today, Rebnok is in the business of ballpoint pens, gel pens and water-colour pens, not fountain pens.

- Sai Pens Private Limited, Bombay
- Sanghvi Ag. Pens Private Limited, Bombay
- Spel Pens Private Limited, Bangalore
- Southern Pencils and Pens Private Limited, Bangalore
- Stylex Pen Company Private Limited, Bombay
- Sunflower Pen Company Private Limited, Bombay
- Toyo Pen Company Private Limited, Bangalore[196]
- Wearever Pens Private Limited, Bombay
- Writewell Pen Company Private Limited, Bombay

---

[195]'About Us', Rebnok, https://bit.ly/3PEeKmj. Accessed on 25 May 2022.
[196]This was incorporated in 1989 and is not to be confused with Toyo Ink.

More importantly, the MCA database does not throw up enterprises that were not incorporated and, therefore, misses out on those brands. With so many pens produced in the small-scale sector, there is no way such a list can hope to be exhaustive. Therefore, one hears of brands that were locally popular and doesn't know much about them. For example, Avdhoot, Blue Nile, Camay, Champak,[197] Chouhan, Cruiser,[198] Everlast, Fellowship, Lazor,[199] Ledo, Lido, Merlin,[200] Pagoda, Parko, Platinex, Plaza, Raja,[201] Realto,[202] Ricoh, Ritter, Sabena, Scout, Swarna and Tiger. In that legacy, one should also mention the traditional network of small-time service centres and service providers who repaired pens, who were also fast dying out. There were artisans and pen-moulders too. Having said this, the list we have compiled from the 1960s and 1970s included the ones mentioned above, and we are inclined to think we have managed to include all the major producers.[203]

---

[197]Delhi Press has a magazine named *Champak*. Except as promotional material with the magazine or for competitions held for children, *Champak* fountain pens were probably never produced.

[198]Not to be confused with the more expensive luxury brand Cruiser

[199]Made by Lazor Hero Pen, Calcutta

[200]A brand from the Rajahmundry region

[201]There were multiple firms that used this brand name.

[202]Manufactured by National Writing Instruments, Mumbai

[203]Please see Appendix III for the full list.

# 7

## COMPETITION, CHURN,
## MAKE AND UNMAKE

The reforms introduced in India since 1991 represented a mindset change—they represented competition. In the first place, QRs on imports and import licensing became untenable, specifically in April 2001. Despite the 1991 reforms, India retained QRs on imports and most of these were for consumer goods. In any event, these QRs were against the thrust of the reforms. They were also incompatible with the GATT, specifically Article XI, which India signed in 1948. However, historically, those QRs were justified through Article XVIII Section B of the GATT, which freed a country from the prohibition on QRs if it was facing BoP problems. In 1999, after a complaint by the US, the World Trade Organization's (WTO) dispute settlement body ruled that given the improvement in India's foreign exchange reserve position, QRs on the grounds of BoP could no longer be justified. India was given till April 2001 to phase out QRs on consumer goods.

For international trade, the harmonized system of customs nomenclature uses digits to denote products. The more the number of digits, the finer the description. In 1999, at the eight-digit harmonized system level of description, there were 2,714 tariff lines subject to QRs on imports, 710 of which were agricultural products. The remainder were industrial products, including consumer goods. After the WTO dispute settlement body's ruling, all these QRs were eliminated in April 2001. In the case of both exports and imports of fountain pens, the numbers are relatively insignificant. At the four-digit harmonized system level, fountain pens figure under the code 9608, along with other kinds of pens. At the six-digit level of 960830, it is either a fountain pen or a stylograph pen. At the eight-digit level of 96083011, it is a high-value fountain pen, costing more than 100 US dollars. At the eight-digit level of 96083012, it is a fountain pen with a body or cap of precious metals. At the eight-digit level of 96083019, it is some other kind of fountain pen.

When QRs on imports are phased out, the focus shifts to tariffs, though protectionism can also surface through non-tariff barriers. At the GATT or WTO, every country sets a maximum tariff rate known as the bound rate. For WTO members, this schedule of concessions means that tariffs can be set no higher than the set bound rate. India's bound rate for fountain pens and similar manufactured products is 43.5 per cent. That is the figure India has indicated to the WTO in the table of tariff concessions after the Uruguay Round. Since this is a cap or ceiling, the actual tariff, known as the applied rate, can be lower. The basic customs duty has been 10 per cent since 2007. Prior to that, it was 52 per cent in 1996, 45 per cent in 1997 and 1998, 40 per cent in 1999, 38.5 per cent in 2000, 30 per cent in 2002 and 2003, 20 per cent in 2004, 15 per cent in 2005 and 12.50 in 2006.[204] In addition to the QR phase out, import duties have also been slashed. Furthermore, there can be additional duties over and above the basic customs duty. To ensure fair competition and a level playing field, imported products should have the equivalent of domestic indirect taxes paid by domestic manufacturers.

## GST and Tariffs

With the introduction of the goods and services tax (GST) in 2017, the domestic indirect tax structure has been vastly simplified, though GST is still a work in progress and needs further simplification. For a start, there still are too many varying GST rates, ranging from 0 per cent to 28 per cent, and not all goods and services are part of the GST framework. For the sake of standardization and simplification, the 0 per cent rate needs to be increased, just as the 28 per cent rate needs to decline. The 45th GST Council meeting, which was held in September 2021, decided to implement a uniform GST of 18 per cent on all pens, removing the bias created towards ballpoint pens, which were taxed at 12 per cent earlier. Ipso facto, the integrated goods and service tax (IGST), applied to import products, also became 18 per cent. The social welfare charge of 10 per cent gets added to this. Briefly, the effective duty imposed on an imported fountain pen (or part) becomes a little more than 31 per cent. Compared to the basic customs duty of 52 per cent in 1996, the basic customs duty is 10 per cent now. The IGST is meant to offset and be equal to domestic

---

[204]These figures have been computed by the authors based on bound rates from WTO schedules and commerce ministry sources.

indirect taxes. Pre-GST, domestic indirect taxes were difficult to compute due to their opaqueness. Clearly, effective import duties have declined. However, an effective import duty of 31 per cent leads to a tendency to evade taxes—both import duties and GST.

This raises some general issues, not specific to fountain pens, which may seem beyond the scope of this book but are crucial to the larger discussion on the economic status of the country. First, GST was meant to be a revenue neutral rate, not one that led to a loss of revenue for central and state governments. The revenue neutral rate was expected to be at least 18 per cent, compared to the present average of around 11.5 per cent. The actual computed revenue neutral rate depends on assumptions made in computation, including assumptions about which products are part of GST. Hence, the numbers vary. However, computations by the Department of Economic Affairs and the National Institute of Public Finance and Policy are in this range.[205] Eventually, when the GST is standardized, it will probably converge to three rates, not one— something like 6 per cent, 12 per cent and 18 per cent, with 6 per cent for merit goods, 12 per cent for standard goods and 18 per cent for demerit goods. Do pens, ballpoint pens and fountain pens deserve to be at 12 per cent or 18 per cent?[206]

---

[205]'Report on the Revenue Neutral Rate and Structure of Rates for the Goods and Services Tax (GST)', Goods and Services Tax Council, 4 December 2015, https://bit.ly/3GLf6Dr. Accessed on 3 June 2022; Mukherjee, Sacchidananda, 'Revenue Implications of GST Rates Restructuring in India: An Analysis', NIPFP Working Paper Series, 15 November 2021, https://bit.ly/3Mjm0RA. Accessed on 3 June 2022.
[206]'GST Rates and HSN Code for Pencils', ClearTax, https://bit.ly/3xanqJU. Accessed on 3 June 2022. The GST rate for pencils is 12 per cent.

That's a call for the GST Council to take.

Second, the social welfare charge is presumably temporary, until indirect tax reform stabilizes and IGST is set to be equal to domestic GST. What should be the basic customs duty on fountain pens? By definition, all tariffs lead to welfare losses for consumers, not adequately compensated by welfare gains to relatively inefficient domestic production. It is not as if the customs duty for imports of fountain pens into the US is 0 per cent. There are bound to be some import duties. Imports can never become completely free.

Assuming that the Indian tariff is to be lowered, should it be done unilaterally or through the quid pro quo of negotiations? Reciprocity is built into international trade negotiations, whether conducted multilaterally through the WTO or through regional trade agreements. By lowering a tariff unilaterally, one loses a bargaining chip that might have been used to extract market access concessions from the trading partner in other sectors. High tariffs can encourage smuggling and under-invoicing and limited quantities of high-value pens can also slink in as personal baggage. At least anecdotally, such smuggling is no longer as rampant as it used to be earlier. The intention is not only to evade customs duties but also IGST and GST, for domestic sales. On the downside, a smuggled pen naturally does not allow the customer to avail of warranty and other services. Tariffs can also encourage FDI in the form of tariff jumping, with greater multiplier benefits for the home country.

Third, ideally, tariffs should be the highest for finished goods, followed by those on intermediates, ending with those on raw materials. For example, if the basic customs duty on fountain pens is 10 per cent, should it be 10 per cent on nibs as well? An inverted duty structure is an issue not only for customs duties but also domestic indirect taxes. Should GST on nibs be 18 per cent, if that on fountain pens is also at 18 per cent? Gold can be used for making fountain pen nibs. If the basic customs duty on fountain pens is 10 per cent, what should it be for gold? Or should one differentiate import duties on gold based on its end use? This can lead to complications and litigation along the lines indicated earlier. The intention is not to provide answers to these questions, but to flag the issues, which are complicated. It is not easy to decide what is a finished good and what is intermediate or raw material.

Simplification requires standardization. Finer distinctions lead to complicated interpretations and litigation. A recent GST advance ruling case from West Bengal, involving Shiva Writing Company Private Limited, will illustrate the point. This entire case is about ballpoint pens, but it illustrates the complexities when there are differing rates. Shiva Writing Company made ballpoint pens and also supplied pen tips and balls to others.

The Applicant seeks a Ruling on

a) Whether tips and ball, both being pen parts under HSN Chapter Head 9608, used in manufacturing process of ballpoint pens, are taxable at the rate of 12%;

b) If the tips and balls used in the manufacturing of ballpoint pens are not taxable at the rate of 12% under HSN 9608, then at what rate shall they be taxable and under which HSN.[207]

---

[207] 'GST: Classification and rate of tax on pen parts', TaxGuru, 13 March 2019, https://bit.ly/3amPDnU. Accessed on 25 May 2022.

In response, the revenue department claimed,

> The 'Ball Point Pens' are classified under Sub-heading no. 960810 of GST Tariff, attracting CGST @6% and SGST @ 6%, while 'Refills for ball point pens, comprising the ball point and ink-reservoir' are classified under Sub-heading no. 960860 of GST Tariff, attracting CGST @ 9% and SGST @ 9%. Tips and balls are the parts of refill, and since there is no specific sub-heading allotted to these parts these may be classified under residuary sub-heading as 'others' in 960899 specifically under Tariff item Sub-heading no. 96089990 of GST Tariff, which attracts GST at a rate of 18% (CGST 9% and SGST 9%).

The ruling deserves to be quoted at length.

> A 'Nib' is the part of a quill, dip pen, fountain pen, or stylus which comes into contact with the writing surface in order to deposit ink. The anatomy of a pen nib is very different from the anatomy of a pen tip [...] A ballpoint pen, on the other hand, is a pen that dispenses ink (usually in paste form) over a metal ball at its point, i.e. over a 'ball point'. The ink is placed in a thin tube whose end was blocked by a tiny ball, held so that it cannot slip into the tube or fall out of the pen [...] So it is evident, that though often used interchangeably by the Applicant, the two words (nib and tip) refer to two different genres and styles of pen in which they are used, with distinctly different ways of channelling the ink. As is clear from the discussion above, 'Nibs' and 'Tips' of pens are completely two different products with distinguishable anatomy catering to different kinds of ink and hence, use. While the split down the centre is the

essential and salient feature of a 'Nib', the ball at the end of the refill is the essential and salient feature of a 'Tip'. The two terms cannot be used synonymously and/or as substitutes of each other.[208]

Had the rates been the same, the scope for subjective interpretation and litigation would not have arisen.

Fourth, while discussing tariffs, it is worth noting that regional trade agreements (RTAs) complicate the argument further, distorting effective rates of protection under a most-favoured nation regime. Nepal has always been a route for smuggled fountain pens to make their way into India. This has been true ever since the 1950 Indo-Nepal Treaty of Peace and Friendship. 'For example, when the Soviet Union and China began to send development aid to Nepal in the early 1950s, donated goods such as cement, sugar, bicycles and fountain pens that were shipped to Kathmandu via India were then promptly smuggled back into the Indian market, where these items had a particular demand.'[209] Furthermore, 'The Nepalese government allows Nepalese exporters to use a percentage of the hard currency they earn to import a variety of goods. Many of these are consumer goods, such as fountain pens, cigarette lighters, transistor radios and motorcycles. Most of these commodities cannot be absorbed by the small Nepalese market and are smuggled into India where they are sold for substantial profits.'[210] As imports have been liberalized in

[208]Ibid.

[209]Zipperer, Kristen, 'Smugglers' Paradise', *Himal Southasian*, 27 May 2013, https://bit.ly/3MNtjlG. Accessed on 25 May 2022.

[210]Gaige, Frederick, 'Nepal: More Problems with India', *Asian Survey*, Vol. 11, No. 2, 1971, https://bit.ly/3yYFLem. Accessed on 25 May 2022.

India and the transaction costs associated with legitimate commercial transactions have declined and those with illegitimate commercial transactions have increased, smuggling of fountain pens no longer occurs on the scale that it used to. The point we are making is more of a pedantic one. If tariffs through RTAs are different from the ones applicable to the most favoured nations, is it at all possible to enforce rules of origin or domestic value addition requirements?

## Surviving the Competition

The message of the 1990s and beyond was one of competition and liberalization, be it through freer imports and FDI, or scrapping of SSI reservations. This happened when the market for fountain pens was already declining, as was the market for writing instruments in general. This last factor is not peculiar to India. There is a paper that explores strategies deployed by Waterman, Montblanc and Parker.

> The paper presents the survival strategies used by three of the most prestigious and ancient fountain pen companies still in activity today [...] Waterman brand is still treasured by collectors and small class of users of high quality pens but by its insertion in a mass market oriented group, it is selling its pens not only in high class outlets as used to be, but also in retailers that can assure more volume of sales [...] As the new millennium opened, Montblanc has a frequently characteristic on launching new collections of writing instruments. Parker's pens are more related to the design and comfort in writing. There are new and recent collections that pay attention

to the ergonomics, design and modern forms to attract young customers.[211]

As this quote illustrates, faced with what the famous economist Joseph Schumpeter called creative destruction, strategies involve not just manufacturing but also marketing, distribution and branding. Fountain pens may have gone into a decline but assessments by industry associations suggest 10 per cent of the Indian writing instrument market still consists of fountain pens. Who caters to that demand and how are Indian fountain pen makers positioned to tap into this? When will there be papers on strategies used by Indian fountain pen makers?

## In Search of the Indian Fountain Pen

Indian fountain pen makers do not belong to a single generation. Pre-Independence manufacturers can be called 1G. In the 1950s and 1960s, it was 2G. The first whiffs of liberalization and the advent of better technology in the late 1970s and 1980s ushered in 3G. 4G manufacturers were those who established their businesses just after the 1991 reforms. One might say that we are still waiting for 5G—a generation that will not only cater to the domestic market but also export overseas. India not only imports pens, it also exports pens. The values are, of course, insignificant, as shown by the Directorate General of Commercial Intelligence and Statistics (DGCI&S). In 2020–21, the value of imports of fountain pens was 2.51 million US dollars,

---

[211]Ferasso, Marcos, Ivan Antonio Pinheiro and Edi Madalena Fracasso, 'Strategies of Innovation in an Ancient Business: Cases of The Fountain Pen Industry', IAMOT Conference Paper, ResearchGate, 2008, https://bit.ly/3lJiIwi. Accessed on 25 May 2022.

a slight dip from the earlier figures ranging between 3 and 3.5 million US dollars. This is for the six-digit code of 960830, which includes not only fountain pens but stylograph pens too. Most imports are from the United Arab Emirates (UAE, read Dubai), followed by China, Germany, Hong Kong, Japan and Taiwan. In 2020–21, the value of exports was 1.58 million US dollars, a slight increase from the earlier figures of around 0.7 million US dollars. The primary export destinations were US, Nepal, Russia, Bangladesh, UK and UAE. Global exports of 960830 are 2982.2 million US dollars, which means India has a 0.05 per cent share of the global export market. Countries with major export shares are Germany, Japan, China, France, Poland, the Czech Republic, Singapore, the UK, Italy and the UAE. For a sense of scale, India's share in global exports of goods is around 1.7 per cent—over 30 times larger than its share in the export of fountain pens. To restate the obvious, India's fountain pen exports perform worse than they should.[212]

If these are countries with major export shares in fountain pens, do they have domestic brands? What are German fountain pen brands? One thinks of Pelikan, Kaweco, Lamy and Montblanc. What are Japanese fountain pen brands? One thinks of Pilot (Namiki), Platinum, Sailor and Taccia. For China, one will think of Huafu (Hero), Jinhao (Baoer), Luoshi, Wing Sung, Moonman and many more. For France, there are Dupoint, Herbin and, now, Parker and Waterman. British brands include Conway Stewart, Diamine and Platignum. Among Italian

---

[212]These figures have been computed by the authors based on data pulled from the following source: 'Directorate General of Commercial Intelligence and Statistics', Ministry of Commerce and Industry, Government of India, https://bit.ly/3mQcI5b. Accessed on 15 June 2022.

brands, there are Aurora, Leonardo, Montegrappa, Scribo, Stipula, Visconti and Wahl-Eversharp. But are there pen brands from Poland, the Czech Republic, Singapore or the UAE?

Once one asks this question, one realizes that the question is misplaced. Exports do not mean a pen is necessarily manufactured in that country—UAE being a case in point. Exports from Singapore do not necessarily mean it is a Singapore-based brand. Pilot (a Japanese brand) may be manufactured through Pilot's subsidiary in Singapore. The nationality associated with a brand can be important but it can also be misleading, as in the earlier anecdote about Wilson nibs being imported. International trade has become more complicated over time. With transportation and logistics becoming easier and associated costs declining, production decisions follow the principles of comparative advantage even more. Therefore, a fountain pen that is completely made within a single country will be extremely rare. Even if such a pen could be made, it would not be economically viable. Hence, there is no such thing as an Indian pen anymore.

In international trade agreements, a concept known as rules of origin is used to determine whether a product has originated within a specific country. When India negotiates a trade agreement, it often uses a 30 per cent value addition criterion. That is, if there is 30 per cent value addition in a product from a country, one can reasonably regard that product as having originated within that country. By the same token, if there is 30 per cent indigenous value addition to a pen, we can regard it as an Indian pen.

Consequently, clips, trim rings, nibs, feeds and converters are imported and so are the resins used to make a pen's body. The capacity to make attractive pens, with designs that customers like, that may be benchmarked against pens made by competitors needs the ability to import material required for the body.[213] In talking about fountain pens, one often forgets that India does make some very good quality nibs, though not in Sattur. Ambitious makes and exports nibs for some of the foremost fountain pen brands in the world. Kanwrite also makes excellent nibs. Earlier, there was a quote about Japanese nibs being among the best in the world. But these (Pilot, Platinum, Sailor) are really made for in-house pens. This is also true of French nibs. Among OEM suppliers of nibs, Kanwrite and Ambitious can hold their own against the best German nib makers—Bock, JoWo, Schmidt. Ditto for ink, with the brands like Bril, Camlin and Daytone.

Among newer inks, one should mention Krishna (started in 2010) and the remarkable Project Syahi, which, as of 2019, seems to have ventured into ink too.

On 19th September 2019, Enactus KMC took a step towards solving the ever-growing problem of single-use plastic pens by launching Project Syahi. 'Syahi', meaning 'ink' in Hindi, is a unique project that renders a business having a crucial impact. Project Syahi creates pens made out of upcycled paper (a waste paper that would have otherwise gone to the dustbin).[214] .

---

[213]India does make and export vegetable resins for pens. But vegetable resins have a distinct smell that not all customers like. Noodler's Ahab sources vegetable resin from India. However, the MSME status of these manufacturers made, and continues to make, import procedures and payment of import duties difficult.

[214]'Syahi Pens Made Out of Upcycled Paper', Prakati, https://bit.ly/3yXpSVi. Accessed on 25 May 2022.

Apart from these ventures, Sulekha ink has also been relaunched. But this is a bit like software. The Indian contribution in a software product is not recognized as Indian until the product and the branding also become Indian. Despite what was said about nothing being truly Indian and made entirely at home, one looks for a brand that is Indian in some sense. This means a retail Indian fountain pen brand, not one where the nib is Indian, or the ink used to write is Indian. This desire will not be completely met even if Pierre Cardin, Reynolds,[215] Schneider, or BIC Cello are eventually made in India.[216]

## Movement Forward

Competition entails exit as well as entry. 1G, 2G and 3G manufacturers have reacted in different ways to competition. One hears more often about their exits. Therefore, with tinges of nostalgia, one reads about the closure of manufacturers like Hilal in Hyderabad, Asoka in Tenali, Misak in Hyderabad and Kale Pens in Pune. Alternatively, one reads about Luxor and manufacturing brands, like Pilot, Waterman and Parker, being under licence, in addition to diversifying from fountain pens to other office supplies. Partly, as a result of the Chellaram family getting divided, Chelpark diversified into not only stationery but also other completely unrelated lines of

---

[215]One could say that Reynolds Pens India Private Limited is in some sense Indian. G.M. Pens used to be a licensee. Fludo is now manufactured by Flair Writing Industries Private Limited.

[216]Cello Pens was founded in 1995 and taken over by BIC in 2015 to become BIC Cello (India). Although they do not just manufacture fountain pens, they still make basic fountain pens.

businesses. However, all of the 1G, 2G and 3G manufacturers have not exited. And contrary to popular belief, there has been quite a bit of entry in pen-making since 1991. Consider the following as a list of examples of the 4G fountain pen sector, spanning across not just manufacturing but also marketing and distribution.

- Aarti Writing Products, based in Gujarat, makes Aarti fountain pens.
- ASA was established in Madras in 2012. ASA[217] stands for Anand, Shruti and Aparnaa Subramaniam.
- Auteur makes a variety of pens.
- Constellations88 was started in Mumbai.
- Fosfor Pens was established in 2014, though there is a long waiting period for their pens.
- Through Fountain Pen Revolution,[218] Kevin Thiemann has popularized sales of many Indian fountain pens abroad, including an in-house brand named Dilli, based out of Delhi. 'I was working in India at the time and, as fate would have it, discovered the world of Indian-made pens.'[219]
- The Fountain Pen Association of India has been formed.
- Before the disruption of the pandemic, an Indian Pen Show was started.

---

[217] ASA is primarily an online marketplace for fountain pens, with in-house brands like Galactic, Nauka, Maya, Genius and Tangerine. It also sells now-defunct brands like Beena. Matipens is another such marketplace.
[218] 'About Us', Fountain Pen Revolution, https://bit.ly/3yVcxgn. Accessed on 25 May 2022.
[219] 'Fountain Pen Revolution', Dromgoole's, https://bit.ly/39Tl9d2. Accessed on 24 May 2022.

- Inked Happiness, a blog, was started a few years ago and is read by every fountain pen lover.
- ITC has started selling Classmate Octane fountain pens.
- Jugraj and Company, based out of Calcutta, sells the Jumax brand of fountain pens.
- Jogmaya Pen Mart, Calcutta, sells Camred fountain pens.
- Krishna Pens, not just ink, are produced by Dr Sreekumar, though there is a long waiting period for these.
- Lotus Pens was started in 2015.
- Magna Carta was founded in Mumbai in 2014.
- Though Makoba's antecedents date back to the 1960s, it is only in the post-1991 era that the brand has become what it is today.[220]
- Modi Senator India Private Limited, a joint venture with Senator, has brought the German Senator brand to India.
- Naresh Pen Company, based out of Delhi, sells Romus fountain pens.
- Oculus Pens Company, based out of Delhi, sells several brands of fountain pens.
- Penhouse was set up in Madras, facilitating online sales.
- Penworld, started in 2013 in Madras, now renamed The

---

[220]Ganguly, Chawm, 'Sripal Jain, Makoba: Fountain Pens, Markets and the New Normal', Inked Happiness, 21 October 2020, https://bit.ly/39OEID8. Accessed on 25 May 2022. 'And every time I answer it kind of takes me back in time and connects me remotely to my forefathers. Makoba is the short name of our Grandfather (that's how he was called in our home town in Rajasthan). Even today, when we visit our home town, our neighbours and well-wishers address us as Makoba's grandsons.'

Pen Store for the World, has changed the way writing accessories are bought, moving purchases online.

- Rytol, an Indo-British joint venture, caters to the luxury segment of fountain pen users.
- Sanay Shah has started Syahi Writing Instruments.
- Scriz pens are made by Turrantbuy.
- Sign Write India Private Limited, based in Mumbai, sells the Orchid brand of fountain pens.
- Submarine, based in Mumbai, makes the Lyra series of fountain pens.
- Swarnalekha, based out of Calcutta, makes not just ballpoint pens but fountain pens too.
- Teuer, based out of Delhi, makes fountain pens.
- Urushi pens[221] are being made in Pune, courtesy Urushi Studio India and G.M. Custom Pens.
- Vazir Fountain Pens was started in Mumbai in 2020.
- William Penn was set up in 2002 and has now acquired Lapis Bard. It has also started Pennline as its own brand.

The point, however, is that barring those who are heavily into fountain pens, few know of these developments.

Here is a question. When was the last time you saw an Indian fountain pen manufacturer come to the market with a new fountain pen, designed and created from the scratch? That is, according to academic experts who have studied the industry segment, the reason why there is zero, I repeat zero R&D, so far as fountain pen turning / manufacture goes [...] The tale of the traditional fountain pen manufacturers—the hand turners, if you may—is

---

[221]These pens are known to have a special Japanese lacquer.

worse. From the repertoire of their grandfathers, the new owners have settled on only a few models, get the parts machined from different OEM operators and are busy raking in the moolah, selling 'hand-made' Indian ebonite abroad, when not creating an artificial demand in the market by restricting supply to jack up prices. They are guilty twice over—once for not doing any R&D whatsoever, but more importantly, for letting the proprietary knowledge of traditional pen making go to waste.[222]

This sounds harsh, but there is no denying that there is more than a grain of truth to this statement.

## A Rundown Industry

Clearly, all is not well with the Indian fountain pen industry. Irrespective of the generation, most Indian fountain pen manufacturers are cottage industries and MSMEs. This leads to problems that are not specific to the fountain pen industry. With the Micro, Small and Medium Enterprises Act of 2006, the historical SSI definition was replaced by the new MSME definition. The 2019–20 Annual Report of MSME ministry stated:

As per the National Sample Survey (NSS) 73rd round, conducted by National Sample Survey Office, Ministry of Statistics & Programme Implementation during the period 2015-16, there were 633.88 lakh unincorporated

[222]Ganguly, Chawm, 'Indian Fountain Pen–Designed from the Scratch, an Oxymoron?' Inked Happiness, 5 September 2021, https://bit.ly/3lJs5fc. Accessed on 25 May 2022.

non-agriculture MSMEs in the country engaged in different economic activities [...] Micro sector with 630.52 lakh estimated enterprises accounts for more than 99% of total estimated number of MSMEs. Small sector with 3.31 lakh and Medium sector with 0.05 lakh estimated MSMEs accounted for 0.52% and 0.01% of total estimated MSMEs, respectively [...] Out of 633.88 MSMEs, there were 608.41 lakh (95.98%) MSMEs were proprietary concerns.[223]

This means that most MSME enterprises lack a legal identity, leading to problems of credit (both working capital and fixed investments), collateral, access to technology and marketing networks and even exit.[224] These problems apply to fountain pens as well. Using the traditional definition, when SSI enterprises faced competition, several of them switched to becoming traders, importing products from China and ceasing manufacture themselves. Places around Shanghai, Yiwu in particular, would be full of such traders. This assertion is about small-scale manufactured items in general, not specifically fountain pens, but it is also true of them. In the cosseted days of lack of competition, there were sellers who actually outsourced production, domestically, and rebranded pens under their own brand names. In the list given above, there are a few who continue to do precisely that, sourcing production not within India, but from China.

---

[223]'Annual Report 2019-20', Ministry of Micro, Small and Medium Enterprises, Government of India, https://bit.ly/3yS6YiK. Accessed on 25 May 2022.

[224]The Insolvency and Bankruptcy Code of 2016 has started to resolve this now. The government's schemes for MSMEs, including marketing, can be found at https://msme.gov.in/#skipCont

Obviously, this is not true of all Indian fountain pen makers, and there are several generations that coexist, including the recent entrants. The average price of a pen is difficult to indicate because the same company can have different models. The cost of the nib will depend on the tip and the plating. A gold nib will be more expensive than a steel one. An eyedropper pen will be cheaper than one that has a converter or a cartridge. An ebonite feeder, which is increasingly rare, will be cheaper than a plastic feeder. The material used in the body also determines the cost. With these qualifications, the prices of Indian pens range from below 100 rupees to over 35,000 rupees.

On a tangential point, there must be a mechanism to fill the ink. The classic filling system was, of course, the eyedropper. With some exceptions of the self-filling type, the second major method of filling a pen is through a converter. The third is a bit like plug and play, with a cartridge. Individuals vary in their preferences. For instance, there is nothing to match the amount of ink an eyedropper fountain pen can hold. However, stains and eyedropper fountain pens often go hand in hand. A cartridge is convenient but may not always be standard. There is also limited flexibility in choice of ink. The choice is fundamentally determined by individual preferences.

Among older Indian fountain pen manufacturers, the default option is often the eyedropper, with ebonite as the material. But not only does ebonite smell, it is also not possible to mould it into attractive designs and colours. Thus, on the nostalgia trip for ebonite, it is important to remember that it has limited USPs and volume. The MSME status of fountain pen manufacturers raises issues of finance, not just for capital investments but also for working capital. Therefore, fountain pens are only manufactured through pre-orders. The manufacturing USP is perceived to be handmade, not large volumes and modern manufacturing. Consequently, quality, consistency, finishing, packaging and branding receive short shrift. Even for the same manufacturer and model, there will be variations, making it difficult for marketing channels to accept production. A lacquer finish, which adds sheen to the pen, costs only about 350 rupees per pen, but only a few Indian manufacturers will bother to do that. Many manufacturers will not have a converter by default and only add it when asked. If a converter is used, it will be of inferior quality, not from Germany (Schmidt). The nib may be inferior. The acrylic may have to come from the US. So, for a decent fountain pen, the import intensity of production can be as high as 70 per cent—not easy for MSMEs to manage.

## Missed Potential

As we have documented, pre-Independence, make in India did exist for fountain pens. However, due to the historical unmake in India policies, make in India did not happen. There are several problems one can identify—distribution issues being one. Few Indian brands feature for sales on the Internet or in stationery shops, like W.H. Smith and high-end, specialized pen shops, like William Penn and Makoba. There used to be traditional distribution networks, with wholesalers offering advances to manufacturers and purchasing the pens. Indian manufacturers have typically not been able to overcome the collapse of this traditional marketing network and its replacement by newer networks, electronic or otherwise. Because of this distribution issue, some manufacturers are hyper-local brands, rather than all-India ones. There are a few Indian companies that have provisions for direct sales to customers through their own websites, with decent payment gateways. It is possible to argue that brick and mortar stationery stores, or even Internet-based channels, charge commissions of 30–40 per cent. But it is also true that the price of many Indian fountain pens is double what it should be.

On a related point, there are some manufacturers that focus more on the overseas market than on the domestic one. One of these pens will sell for 6,000 rupees in India, but for over 10,000 rupees in the US. Hence, one understands the preference. Oddly enough, very few Indian brands focus on the 2,000–5,000 rupees segment, which is fast-growing. This is where a brand like TWSBI dominates. For more than five decades, Ta Shin Precision was an OEM manufacturer for global brands, before TWSBI was established as its brand. Unlike India, TWSBI's moulding facilities are state of the art, large-scale and modern, something that India should have been able to achieve, both in OEM and branding, given its traditional expertise and considering the fact that Taiwan had no tradition in fountain pen making. For that matter, Jin Gi Industrial Company, Penlux and International Writing Instrument Corp. (I.W.I.C.), all Taiwanese companies, have done the same for turning. Therefore, such OEM work goes to Taiwan. Turkey also did not have any tradition in making fountain pens. Yet, Scrikks (established in 1963, with the first fountain pen produced in 1966) has become a brand and sells much more in the Indian market in the 1,000–2,000 rupees band than Indian brands. With the caveats we have mentioned earlier, there is no reason why a decent Indian fountain pen should not be sold in the 2,000–5,000 rupees segment.

It is possible to argue that a comparison with Chinese pens is unfair because China is not quite a market economy and their pricing policies are not transparent. Anti-dumping duties, when imposed, are a fair indication of the extent to which Chinese prices are unfair at the cross-border level.[225] The average anti-dumping duty imposed on Chinese products, not fountain pens, is to the order of 25 per cent.[226] Even if one accepts the argument that this only reflects non-transparent pricing at the border, and not internally, the unfairness argument should not translate to the kind of pricing that Indian pens have, when decent Chinese pens, not even fancy ones, are available for less than 1,000–2,000 rupees. Part of the problem here is the general bane of Indian manufacturing, with a litany of generic problems—complicated procedures, taxation, availability and cost of physical infrastructure (including logistics and power), cost and availability of credit, land and labour-related issues, etc. At that generic level, government initiatives are intended to solve these and encourage make in India.[227]

The scenario for fountain pens is only partly bleak.

Indian pen making Industry has been around for almost 7 decades now and for most of the time it has been stagnant without much innovation in products or manufacturing technology. I believe the Indian fountain pen industry is witnessing the growth like that of a bamboo tree, which

---

[225] An anti-dumping duty is imposed on an exporting enterprise, not a country, when exports occur at lower than the 'normal value', which is variously defined.

[226] This figure has been calculated based on: 'Anti-Dumping Duty Notifications', Central Board of Indirect Taxes and Customs, https://bit.ly/3mQ3CW5. Accessed on 15 June 2022.

[227] For more details, see: Make in India, https://bit.ly/3NKWTZF. Accessed on 13 June 2022.

grows patiently underground for the longest time to build stronger roots and suddenly spurts up from nowhere [...] Many Indian fountain pen brands have adopted modern technologies and use of imported key parts like the nib and the convertors. Indian pens have quite some distance to travel before competing with International brands, especially in the areas of fine finishes and R&D in design, mass production and marketing. I believe the journey is at its last leg and now it is turn of the Indian fountain pen user to recognize good Indian fountain pens and support them and push them and motivate them to take the next leap.[228]

The catch is the constraints placed by the products being handmade and manufactured by MSMEs. This is the reason the recent developments and brands that have been launched have been about talking to each other and preaching to the converted, with a distinctly incestuous tinge. The conversion to a mass market is yet to happen. The protective policies we have documented in this book, highlighting unmake, have not encouraged this.

At the risk of subjectivity, there are a few in the present lot that can take Indian fountain pens to that 5G stage, recognizing the many transitions India is going through—from formal to informal, unorganized to organized and MSME to large-scale. The transition to modern fountain pen manufacturing is still a work in progress. Airmail or Wality are flattered to deceive. In our subjective identification, we think Click, V-Sign, Kanwrite

---

[228]Ganguly, Chawm, 'Sripal Jain, Makoba: Fountain Pens, Markets and the New Normal', Inked Happiness, 21 October 2020, https://bit.ly/3LSpavC. Accessed on 25 May 2022.

and Vazir have the potential to make that transition, with Ambitious thrown in, if it chooses to make that transition to fountain pens. We will be happy to be proved wrong and delighted if there are many more. The churn is real. Make in India beckons. At some indeterminate date in the future, there may be an Indian fountain pen that will script that story and make it global.

# APPENDIX I

List of producers from the *Report on the Fountain Pen Ink Industry August 1949*,[229] Board of Trade, 1950:

1. A.P. Industries (Bombay);
2. Alayam's Industries (Coimbatore);
3. Alpha Ink Manufacturing Company (Palghat);
4. Alpha Trading and Manufacturing (Kanpur);
5. Ashar Ink Company (Jalgaon);
6. Asoka Inks (Tenali);
7. Athene's Products (Madras);
8. PM Bagchi and Company Limited (Calcutta);
9. A.C. Banerji (Calcutta);
10. S. Bandye and Company (Calcutta);
11. Bharat Carbon and Ribbon Manufacturing (Calcutta);
12. V.K. Bhat (Poona);
13. Bishop and Company (Calcutta);
14. Blitz Products (Baroda);
15. Calcutta Miscellany (Calcutta);
16. Camlin (Bombay);
17. Chemproducts (Calcutta);
18. The Cottage Ink Industry (Kadiri, Madras);

---

[229]"Report on the Fountain Pen Ink Industry August 1949", Indian Culture, 1949, https://bit.ly/3xAvAeN. Accessed on 9 June 2022.

19. Dayalbagh Chemical Works (Agra);
20. Dayalbagh Ink Factory (Coconada, Madras);
21. Duro Chemical Works (Calcutta);
22. Dye Products Company (Calcutta);
23. Ever Ready Fountain Pen Ink (Madras);
24. Free India Industries (Gudur, Madras);
25. Full Moon Chemical Works (Howrah);
26. G. & B. Industrial Syndicate (Calcutta);
27. The General Essentials Manufacturing Company (Bangalore);
28. R. R. Gobson (Bombay);
29. Gripex (Calcutta);
30. Gurukul Chemical Industries (Hardwar [now Haridwar]);
31. Hairhar Research Works (Ahmedabad);
32. India Ink and Chemical Industries (Lucknow);
33. Indian Universal Industries (Delhi);
34. Industrial Research House (Allahabad);
35. Sham Chand Jain and Sons (Delhi);
36. Jesco Industrials and Agencies (Trivandrum);
37. Kala Products (Madras);
38. Kale's Ink Manufacturing Company (Bombay);
39. Karkhanis Brothers (Jodhpur);
40. B. Karr and Company (Calcutta);
41. Kempanwar Chemical Works (Hubli, Dharwar);
42. Keshava Picture Mart (Bulandshahr);
43. Kohinur Industrials (Kallianpur, South India);
44. Krishnaveni Inks (Madras);
45. K.V. and Sons (Bellary, Madras);
46. Lahore Stationary Mart (Delhi);
47. Dr R.K. Lal and Sons (Benares);
48. Lily Chemical Works (Calcutta);

49. McPhall's Trading Company (Bombay);
50. McPhall's Trading Company (South India);
51. National Products Syndicate (Madras);
52. Navele Brothers (Bangalore);
53. Neel Kaal Inks (Tenali, Madras);
54. Pillet Ink Company (Calcutta);
55. Prabhu's Ink (Katalur, Madras);
56. Profile Limited (Calcutta);
57. Radio Ink Manufacturing (Madras);
58. Raman Inks Company (Madras);
59. G.S. Ranade and Company (Bombay);
60. Rangoon Miscellany (Calcutta);
61. Ray Brothers (Calcutta);
62. Rapido Industries (Calcutta);
63. Ravi Inks (Madras);
64. Raz Brothers (Calcutta);
65. Research Chemical Laboratories (Madras);
66. Royal India Industries (Baroda);
67. Sinde and Company (Poona);
68. Shelat Brothers (Madras);
69. Sheth and Company (Bombay);
70. Shreyakar's Student Ink Manufacturing Company (Belgaum);
71. C.N. Subramaniam (Madras);
72. Sulekha Works Limited (Calcutta);
73. Stewart Laboratories (Bombay);
74. T.S. Research Laboratory (Calcutta);
75. Techno Chemical Industries (Madras);
76. Techno Chemical Industries (Calcutta);
77. True Ink Manufacturing Company (Calcutta);
78. Unita Trading Company (Calcutta);

79. Valji and Company (Gadag);
80. Victory Soap Works (Ulundurpet, South India);
81. N. Vishwanathan Iyer (Madras);
82. Zenith Ink and Gum Products (Calcutta).

# APPENDIX II

With the vintage of the 1950s and 1960s, the following is an alphabetical list of fountain pen producers. This list has been drawn up by trawling the trademark database,[230] though it is impossible to make it exhaustive. It inevitably excludes producers who did not bother to get their brands registered.

- Airmail and Wality: Airmail Pen Company was established in 1951 by Mohan L. Mirchandani. It has two brands—Wality and Airmail that are manufactured even today.
- Ambassador: In 1963, General Pen Agencies registered and marketed the Ambassador brand of fountain pens in Chandigarh. This brand later diversified to ink as well.
- Artex, Flora and Kingson: Artex Pen Mart, Calcutta, launched the Artex brand in 1959. The brand was owned by Purshottam Das Sethi, who subsequently re-registered the trademark under S.P. Industries, which was co-owned by him. As Sethi Pen Store, Sethi also registered the brand Flora, later re-registered as Artex Pen Mart. These legal niceties apart, Artex fountain pens were extremely popular, especially in the eastern parts of the country, along with parallel brands like Flora, B-tex, Garden, and Primax. These

---

[230]'Public Search of Trade Marks', Ministry of Commerce & Industry, Government of India, https://bit.ly/3QkYlU5. Accessed on 15 June 2022.

brands were not manufactured in-house. Instead, production was outsourced to small, local artisans. Subsequently, the family added a Kingson brand to the portfolio.

- Bachelor: Rajpal Gambhir registered this trademark in Calcutta in 1960. Anecdotal reports suggest that this brand used to be popular in the 1960s.
- Beena: In 1965, Satramdas Bikhachand Motwani established the Beena Pen Company. The brands Beena Magic, Beena Lincoln and Beena Chaplin were fairly popular.

> It began more than five decades back in 1965 when Satramdas Motwani went into the manufacturing of fountain pens and established, what has now become, the legacy brand—Beena. It wasn't long before he was sought after— because of his vast, hands-on knowledge about manufacturing in general and fountain pens in particular. Naturally, it wasn't long again, before he had become a supplier of choice to most of the major brands of the day. Some Beena models, like the Magic and Lincoln, it will not be an exaggeration to state, had even attained near cult status and are still highly prized by collectors.[231]

Beena was also an OEM supplier for brands like Camlin and Chelpark. For a while, as OEM supplies drove the market, their own brands were neglected. However, in the last decade, Beena has been revived under the Beena Antic and V'sign brands.

- Cadet: In the 1960s, Bhaiya Industries from Indore

---

[231]Ganguly, Chawm, 'Beena—The Kal, Aaj Aur Kal of Indian Fountain Pens', Inked Happiness, 7 February 2021, https://bit.ly/3sXRlTb. Accessed on 25 May 2022.

manufactured Cadet fountain pens and sold them through Bhaiya Stores, based out of Indore.

- Caravan: In 1954, Sadhuram T. Khilnani registered this brand of fountain pens and later extended it to fountain pen nibs and ink.
- Cato: This brand was marketed in late 1940s and early 1950s by Continental Metal and Plastic Industries, Bombay.
- Champion: Gujarat Industry Private Limited, based out of Bombay, launched this brand in the early 1950s and sold it for more than two decades.
- Diploma and Diplomat: In 1957, United Pen Mart launched the Diploma brand of fountain pens in Calcutta, followed by the Diplomat brand in the 1960s.
- Doctor and Maxy: In the early 1960s, Motiram Khilnani established M.H. Products in Bombay and launched the Doctor and Maxy brands. These brands were registered as trademarks, not only for fountain pens but also for ballpoint pens.
- Dutson: Dutta Pen and Sports House registered this trademark for fountain pens and ballpoint pens in 1967 in Calcutta, a brand name that got extended to unrelated products as well.
- Hamraj: In 1968, Hem Raj, from Benares, registered a Hamraj trademark for fountain pens and ink. The trademark continued with Hem Raj Trading, which is operating as Delhi Pen House. The Hamraj brand was especially popular in Uttar Pradesh through, for instance, the Hamraj Pen Store in Benares.[232]

---

[232]This should not be confused with Hamraj pencils, a brand sold by Paradise Pencils and Paradise Traders.

- Kim, Kriptok, Amber, Elite: There was a cottage industry of sorts in Calicut (now Kozhikode). As in some earlier examples, M. Haneefa Rawthar used to sell fountain pens there. Perforce, he had to start repairing them and Kim and Company was set up as a repairing centre in 1942. In 1955, Kim and Company started manufacturing fountain pens. Calicut did not become a centre for fountain pen manufacture only because of Kim and Company. There were three others: Kriptok, Amber and Elite. However, the model was the same—retail and servicing outlets and manufacturing a small number of in-house fountain pens. There were close links between Kim, Kriptok, Amber and Elite. Later, Amber Pens changed its name to Krishna Pens.
- Misak: Those from Hyderabad still rave about Kasim Hasan Kham's Misak Pen Store and the Misak brand (Misak was Kasim written in reverse). The trademark was registered in 1956.
- Murphy and Radar: R.P. Traders, owned by the Narula family still exists in Calcutta and is a wholesale supplier of fountain pens and fountain pen ink. In the late 1960s, they briefly sold the Murphy and Radar brands.
- Nataraj and Apsara: Hindustan Pencils Private Limited was established in 1958 and has a significant presence in the pencil and school stationery market. Today, it also produces pens, but those are ballpoint and gel pens. However, in 1969, the Nataraj trademark was also registered (in Bombay) for fountain pens.
- Pamis: This was a brand registered in Bombay in 1962 in the name of Kishinchand Radhakrishin Chandiramani.
- Pearl and Pearl Stylo: Marketed in the 1950s by Nilmoni Halder and Company, Calcutta, these pens were probably

not manufactured but outsourced and rebranded.

- Prasad: This brand was started in Tenali by Kanneganti Prasad Rao in 1954 and the Prasad Pen Company was eventually sold in 1977. Some popular Prasad brands include the Prasad Duofold, Prasad Major, Prasad Medium and Prasad Baby.
- Rekha: Many years ago, this used to be a popular fountain pen brand in Maharashtra and was registered in 1961 by Popular Pen and Clip Industries.
- Rite Sharp: The Rite Sharp Pen Company launched this brand, which seems to have done well locally.
- Sevika: This was probably a very local brand. In 1961, Exen Industries registered this trademark in Bombay for fountain pens and parts.
- Sunkrist: Rajaram R. Ahuja registered this trademark in Bombay in 1963. Sunkrist fountain pens (along with ballpoint pens) and ink were common in Maharashtra.
- Switch: This seems to have been a brand used by Paradise Pen Company Private Limited, incorporated in Bombay in 1968.
- Titoni: In 1961, Suresh Banerjee started producing the Titoni brand of fountain pens, fountain pen parts and fountain pen ink in Calcutta.
- Titus: In 1966 Bombay Fountain Pen Depot registered and launched the Titus brand of fountain pens and parts in Bombay.
- Visitor: This is a brand name for fountain pens and parts that few remember now. Kundu and Basak Industries registered this trademark in Calcutta in 1964.
- Westend: In 1960, Srichand and Brothers registered this brand name in Calcutta for fountain pens and parts.

Westend Duralex used to be a locally popular brand.

- Youth: This was a brand for fountain pens and parts registered by Triplex Products in Bombay in 1968.
- Winner: In 1966, Navin Chandra Chandulal and Company registered and launched the Winner brand of fountain pens and parts in Madras.

# APPENDIX III

Given below is a list of fountain pen producers from the 1970s and 1980s:

- Abhay Pen Agency in Aurangabad started as a dealer of fountain pens in 1971 and eventually started making the Mohi brand of ebonite and acrylic pens, which are still produced.
- Arora Pen Agencies sold the Hema brand in Andhra Pradesh.
- Bhimraj and Company, Madras, was set up in 1971 and introduced the Oliver brand.
- Corvina was a brand produced by R.K. Dhoka in Mumbai.
- G.M. Pens International Private Limited was set up in Delhi in 1986 and sells the Rorito and Prido brands today.
- In the 1970s, in Pune, Murlidhar Gopal Kale started the Kale Pen Company, which produced Kale fountain pens, nibs and ink. Kale no longer sells fountain pens, a fact rued by the older residents of Pune. It still sells inks and nibs though. They used to sell their ink in plastic bags.

  During the glory days, the owner would display the different coloured [fountain pen] models and the customer would choose their favourite one. Mr Kale would then assemble the pen right in front of their eyes. With several branded pens and stationery items now in the market, it's pretty clear that this small yet humble pen shop is fast approaching its last breath. A tragic end of an era; all good things must end unfortunately. However, their pens will still etch fond memories in our minds and hearts.[233]

This story has been replicated in many parts of India.

- Kanpur Writers or Kanwrite (under the fountain pen brand names of Heritage and Desire) was established in 1986. Though Kanwrite does make fountain pens, it is known more as a producer of nibs and is one of those rare instances of a nib manufacturer also making pens. For example, among German nibs, JoWo and Bock make excellent nibs, but they do not make fountain pens. As a counter-argument, one can, of course, cite Lamy, Pelikan or Sailor. The founder of Kanwrite, Sandeep Awasthi, in an interview, tells us both about Kanpur Writers and the predicament of the industry, which justifies a long quote.

  When we had started, Kanpur Writers made only Fountain Pen nibs and our production was approximately 30-40 thousand pieces per day. During those days, other major producers together made another 2.0 Lakh units per day (approximately). In the present, either most of them have closed down or have reduced production substantially and the total production is less than 1.0 lakh units per day. We enjoy approximately 40 % share of the current production, our output primarily targeted, en mass, to the premium

[233]Burange, Yashodhaan, 'A Tribute to Pune's Kale Pens', *The Punekar*, 1 April 2018, https://bit.ly/38hsO4d. Accessed on 25 May 2022.

segment of the market [...] In the beginning, we used to manufacture only Fountain Pen nibs. However, as the market for nibs contracted, we diversified into Fountain Pen making, initially supplying to a big entity based out of Mumbai. It wasn't before long that we realised that in the domestic market, there is a distinct cap and up-scaling in terms of better quality or price was not an easy option. It was then that we decided to develop International OE customers. In number terms, we can say that 70 % of our sales comes from International market (including FP and Nibs) and rest comes from our domestic sales of Kanwrite brand products + domestic OE nib sales [...] We started exporting our products from year 2000 and really got entranced in the market from 2010 on-wards. As to comparing our products with those made in other countries, one should remember that there are only 4 countries that are producing nibs in an organised way: Germany—traditionally the best in terms of quality but very expensive in terms of cost, Japan—next only to Germany but also very expensive. I am not aware if they sell nibs to third parties as spares. India—we offer the best value for money, and, China—they offer nibs at the cheapest price points but there are no guarantees about quality. As a matter of fact, their quality is so poor that no one can predict that out of 100 nibs in a box how many will run satisfactory [...] If we tell the truth, our launching of the Kanwrite brand in India was a pleasant accident. Although we had registered our brand much earlier, we had not really thought of launching our line of fountain pens, keeping the idea in the back-burner. As a matter of fact, when we came to know that many Indian collectors were importing our products by paying heavy Customs Duties, we decided to make some products available in the local market, purely as a test case. In a way, we are still pretty low on the learning curve about the retail market for fountain pens.[234]

Some of the problems include,

Non-availability of Good quality Trims and Ebonite rods, Very high custom duties and GST in comparison to China, US or Europe. The biggest irony is that on Ball pens (which generates a lot of plastic and pollutants harmful to the environment and have huge carbon footprints) GST is 12% while on Fountain Pen (which is re-usable, mostly Bio degradable, eco-friendly and sustainable) it's 18%. No known institute or Technical establishment or Government Organisation exists which can support or provide the R&D support to MSMEs of this sector.[235]

- Mebsons from Mumbai started in the 1980s and fizzled out in the late 1990s, diversifying into other lines of business. Starting with ballpoint pens (somewhat unusual), Mebsons moved into fountain pens, exporting to many countries.

---

[234]Ganguly, Chawm, 'Kanpur Writers—The Story of India's Largest Manufacturer of Fountain Pen Nibs', Inked Happiness, 29 July 2020, https://bit.ly/38HQu25. Accessed on 25 May 2022.

[235]Ibid. The GST rates for both ball pens and fountain pens have now been unified at 18 per cent.

Mebsons fountain pens had lacquer and gold coating, which was unusual for the times (outside of Japan). Their brand names included Mebsons, Alisons, Persia and Corvina.

- Montex Pen (India) Private Limited was set up in 1976 but initially not as a corporate entity. That happened much later, in 2006. The brand Montex was not meant only for fountain pens and parts but also for ballpoint pens, ink, other writing instruments and stationery products. Indeed, Montex started off by manufacturing nibs. Though Montex has now diversified into making ballpoint pens and gel pens, it still has fountain pen brands like Handy, Student, Montee, Study and Story.
- Officer: Kartar Singh registered the Officer brand In Chandigarh.
- Peebee Industries sold the Sangeeta brand of fountain pens and parts in Maharashtra, Andhra Pradesh and Mysore.
- Newton: Calcutta Plastic Industries sold this brand of fountain pens and ballpoint pens, which were probably only sold locally.
- Nitu and Serwex: Through Mehra Sales and Service, Ram Kumar Mehra launched the Nitu fountain pen brand in Himachal Pradesh and its sales soon extended to Punjab, Haryana, Uttar Pradesh, Rajasthan and Delhi. Ram Kumar Mehra's subsequent brand, Serwex, which was based in Delhi, is better known. Serwex fountain pens and nibs are still occasionally available.
- Pratap: This was a trademark registered to Virendra Kumar Roshanlal Makol and the Pratap fountain pen brand, based out of Baroda. It was popular in the western parts of the country.
- Radhi Kum, now in the cosmetics business, sold the Libra

brand of fountain pens and ink in Tamil Nadu.

- Ranga Pens was established in 1970 by M.S. Pandurangan in Thiruvallur or Tiruvallur. Why Thiruvallur? The answer is obvious enough—easy availability of ebonite and there used to be a cottage industry of small fountain pen makers in and around Thiruvallur, three or four of which were major. Of these, Oswal Pen Company, which started in the 1940s and closed down in 1965, was the most important. Thus, Oswal pre-dated Ranga.

> We don't use Lathe, we just cut pen threads by hand chasing. It requires 20 years of experience for normal man to practice it. It is followed only in Japan now... Then we slowly moved to machines. We made thousands of celluloid (Cellulose Nitrate) pens in our early days [...] There has been huge demand for our products as they are completely handmade.[236]

While that handmade bit can be a USP, it can also become a weakness.

- Sagar Pen House, Agra, produced the Sagar, Navyug and Medico brands.
- Sakti Mantle, Calcutta, owned the Sakti brand of fountain pens and ballpoint pens, which were probably only sold locally.
- Shah Pen and Plastic Industries, Ahmedabad, sold a Sonet brand of fountain pen and nibs, which were probably only marketed locally.
- Suresh Pen House produced the Winstar brand of fountain

---

[236]'About Us', Ranga Pens, https://bit.ly/3Gfycl5. Accessed on 25 May 2022.

pens and parts in Tamil Nadu.

- Syed Agencies in Ernakulam made Bismipens, a brand registered as a trademark in 1975. This company was established by Haji S. Mohammed Bismi in 1970 and was quite a rage until the end of the 1980s, with the brand also extending to ballpoint pens, until Bismi eventually closed down. When the older pen companies from Kerala went into a decline, along with Bismi, the Jubilee brand, produced in Kunnamkulam, was fairly popular in the 1970s.
- Teko Pen Industries, Calcutta, registered a Teko trademark and sold a William brand of fountain pens.
- Unique Pen Industries (the Click brand) was established in Indore in 1978. There are pens made for collectors and there are pens made for actual use. The two do not always match.

> Jowo or Schnider? Who cares? Nicco ebonite? [...] The one pen that rules the roost in this end of the market is the Aristocrat from Click. As a matter of fact, I will go to the extent of unequivocally proclaiming that (and I am sure that my peers in the fountain pen fraternity will agree) the best entry level fountain pen in India is the Aristocrat from Click. It is. And it has been the best since the time it was launched around 2016.[237]

Any user of functional fountain pens will agree with this assessment. Click also makes ebonite pens and calligraphy pens, apart from producing pens on OEM basis. No fountain

---

[237]Ganguly, Chawm, 'Aristocrat from Click—The Best Entry Level Pen in India', Inked Happiness, 15 August 2020, https://bit.ly/3NBzVDO. Accessed on 25 May 2022.

pen user will dispute that assertion about Aristocrat and, slightly higher up the price ladder, will probably mention the Falcon and Century brands.

- Vikram: In Nagpur, Arjandas M. Ahuja sold fountain pens, ballpoint pens and ink under the brand names Vikram, Ajax and Galaxy. However, these were probably only sold locally.

# INDEX